MILTON CANIFF'S
A ★ M ★ E ★ R ★ I ★ C ★ A

REFLECTIONS OF A
DRAWINGBOARD
P A T R I O T

Edited by Shel Dorf

INTRODUCTION

Since 1975 I have lettered-out Milton Caniff's Christmas day strips. When the pencilled strip arrives at my San Diego, California studio from New York it is a magic moment. I'm the first one to read it. Then I take out pen and ink and carefully letter Mr. Caniff's words which millions of newspaper readers will see on December 25th.

These special strips have always been important to me. Back when I was a young comic strip fan in Detroit, I'd go downtown to buy the December 25th issue of every out-of-town paper I could find. On that day the comic pages were bursting with love and good will. Each cartoonist did something special. But it was a certainty that the most moving message was from Milton Caniff. It usually had to do with the sacrifices made by our military to protect freedom and the importance of keeping our guard up. It made us grateful and proud to be Americans. By choosing that approach on the special day of peace, Mr. Caniff validates his patriotism and helps us validate ours.

Expanding on the patriotism theme we have included the work he has done for the Air Force, Boy Scouts, public service drawings and a sequence from the Steve Canyon strip. Considering the span of the Caniff career and how much in demand he is, plus the fact that he seldom said "no," there is much material to include. We hope you like what I have selected.

SHEL DORF, Editor

Published by Eclipse Books, P.O. Box 1099, Forestville, CA 95436. (707) 887-1521   ISBN 0-913-035-25-4. All artwork ©1987 Milton Caniff. "Drawingboard Patriot" text ©1987 Chris Jensen. "Tribute" text ©1987 Catherine Yronwode. All other text ©1987 Shel Dorf.

JAMES STEWART

The newspaper cartoonist is not unlike an actor, giving life to his characters
both in word and illustration. One of our
greatest practitioners of this art is Milton
Caniff. We've seen that famous boxed signature
in our newspapers over fifty years now. Caniff
uses dialogue well. I am often moved by what
he has to say when he touches upon patriotism.
His viewpoint of America at its best gives us
a standard to show our future generations.

I am happy that this book is being
done as a way to preserve his good words.

Best regards,

James Stewart

TRIBUTE

Milton Caniff is indisputably one of the greatest—and most influential—cartoonists ever to have put pen to paper. His reputation rests upon his rock-solid draftsmanship, his astounding development of the *chiaroscuro* inking technique (which he, in fairness, is always quick to credit to his late studio partner Noel Sickles, who pioneered—and then abandoned—the style), and his marvelously detailed story-lines, filled with the passions, complexities and emotional insights of high literature.

To those unfamiliar with Caniff's work, it may seem folly to invoke a word like "literature" in reference to newspaper comic strips. Suffice it to say that one of the things which distinguishes high literature from low soap opera is a concern with the larger issues in society and in life, and Caniff delivers these in spades. Unlike most other adventure strip authors, Caniff has never limited himself to boy-meets-girl, two-girls-love-same-boy, and good-guy-avenges-death-of-his-buddy stories. Sure, his tales contain elements of those eternal situations, but they are always seen as part of a larger, denser tapestry of human aspiration, failure and triumph.

Chief among the "larger issues" Caniff has tackled are world political events and the way they affect individuals. Seemingly bent on breaking the old adage which advises against discussing politics or religion with anyone outside one's own sect or party, he has made the former, at least, his particular domain, and has never feared to express his beliefs in print.

This is not to say that Caniff has ever endorsed one political party over another, or advocated an agenda beyond that of patriotic commitment to democracy; rather he has celebrated the unifying love of country, and pointed with somber reflection to the lives which must be sacrificed in times of war to preserve our nation's integrity.

Now this may seem a little thing to espouse, patriotism, but in political debate even the simplest concept can be twisted and turned to uses far afield from its original meaning. During World War Two, when our allies were literally fighting for their lives, when our people had been killed in a sneak attack, when fascist aggression threatened this nation's very existence, it was easy to agree on a definition of patriotism: it meant the defense of our borders, of our people, and of our democracy. And this period, not so coincidentally, coincided with Caniff's greatest popularity. The nation at war *needed* a beautifully drawn, artfully plotted dramatic comic strip which bolstered morale while never shirking from truthful depiction of the personal tragedies of warfare—and Milton Caniff delivered.

If war unites us in patriotic activity, then it can be said that times of peace bring us the greatest disagreements on the subject of patriotism. Patriotism in times of peace can run the gamut from love of one's country, its geography, its natural resources, its people, and its government to military preparedness, nuclear stockpiling, covert acts of destabilization against unaligned nations, armed aggression against weakly developed or globally unimportant nations, and, ultimately, blind obedience to authority which will brook no controversy, even in the name of the democratic process.

Patriotism without a war of survival to give it focus and purpose becomes a slippery, complex concept suitable for use in various corrupt ways. In the hubbub and tumult of our democratic decision-making, it is easy to lose patience with "the other side"—and just as easy to lose one's temper. Internal policy debates become bitter feuds when the word "patriotism" is invoked by both sides to the issue: The McCarthy hearings, the undeclared war in Viet Nam, the scandal of Watergate, the "secret team" which carried out military and intelligence work contrary to the rulings of Congress—it doesn't matter which side you take on these issues, someone is bound to speak up for the other side and say you are not "patriotic," while your side is busy condemning their side for the same fault.

Milton Caniff, as a free-speaking patriot, chose long ago to embed certain political beliefs within the framework of his adventure stories. Without the protective indulgence granted to editorial cartoonists by partisan newspapers, he willingly has spoken his piece and stood up to the criticism of those who disagree with his opinions. Disagreement of this sort is not viewed lightly in the newspaper business, for it can lead to a loss of circulation, which is deadly, so one must credit Caniff not only with honesty, but with economic bravery.

The extent of this economic bravery may be judged by the following: In 1967 i—who had followed the adventures of Terry Lee and Pat Ryan with a lump in my throat and pride in my American breast, who had read more than one of Caniff's post-war Christmas episodes through tear-filled eyes—wrote an angry letter to my local paper promising never to look at *Steven Canyon* again because i felt Caniff was conflating the worthy issue of military preparedness with America's unworthy armed assault upon a tiny South-East Asian country that had not attacked us in any way and with which we were not formally at war. Those were tough times for people on both sides of the fence, and Caniff has commented that he "lost a generation of readers" over his outspoken beliefs. He certainly lost me—for about five years.

Of course that is all in the past now, and the mudslinging is over. Caniff returned to my daily must-read list as soon as the Viet Nam conflict was ended and he stopped making fun of long-haired "protesters." In the 1980s we began to correspond a little (with me saving every note he sent!) and eventually we even met. One of the greatest honours in my life has been my fragile friendship with this towering genius of sequential art—and the preservation of his artistic legacy in book form has long been one of my fondest goals. The publication of this collection has given me a chance to participate toward that important end.

Caniff's love of America verges on the holy. When he speaks of defending our liberty, he embues his work with an emotional rawness that can rip a reader out of a comfortable easy chair and into the heat of battle. When he beats the drums of martial might, he never forgets that essential downward minor chord that speaks of death and loss and loneliness. He is a patriot, an orator, an image-maker, and a mythologizer of America at is best, as it should be, and perhaps once was.

Knowing how powerful his prose and art had been in support of our military during both war and peace (and i hope Milton understands this), it was with trepidation that i read for the first time those Viet Nam era strips i had forsworn, as they were assembled for this collection. I think what i feared was renewed exposure to the divisiveness and name-calling which had wracked the country then. Or, to put it in precisely personal terms, i feared i would be forced to confront an arbitrary and absolute definition of patriotism given by the hand of a man whom i respect—a definition calculated to cast doubt upon the loyalty of those who stood on the other side of a certain fence. After all, i am a patriot too, even though we could not agree in 1967 just what that meant.

Did i find what i feared? No, not really. I found commitment, and honest opinion, and even a little sarcasm. I found compassion, and adherence to principles, and a willingness to risk public disapproval by openly advocating deeply held beliefs. I found, in short, exactly what's inside of me too, the mainspring that keeps my love of this country going.

It may sound trite, but i discovered more than a piece of Milton Caniff i had overlooked during that half-decade—i discovered again what it's all about, this America of ours: In times of decision, we are all obliged to speak our pieces. The only person who is NOT a patriot is the one who will not take part in the democratic process.

catherine yronwode

Early Work

Milton at age 8.

FIRST SERIES

The above cartoon was done by 12 year old Milton Caniff, who even at that tender age worried about the "Bulsheviks."

CHIC AND NOODLES - - - - - - - - By Milt Caniff

For his high school paper.

JUNIOR-SENIOR GIRLS TOLD OF CONFERENCE

Plans and Program for Vocational Meeting Related

An assembly for junior and senior girls was held last Wednesday dur- ᵃ fth period in the auditor- ⁻⁻ᵐ for the fifth an- ⁻⁻ch 28, was an- 'v Prepared," '⁻ of the

MUSICAL NUMBERS OF "GOING UP"

ACT I.

Overture	Orchestra
1. Opening Chorus	Mabel Mehaffee, Alwylda Holsapple, Hazel Kiefauver, Bell Boys and First Chorus
2. I'll Bet You	Harry Becker, First Chorus
3. Linger Awhile	Hazel Kiefauver, Bell Boys
4. I Want a Boy	Doris Wetzel, Milton Caniff and the Four Suitors
5. If You Look In Her Tyes	Doris Wetzel, Florenceada Gandre, M. Mehaffee
6. Going Up	Henry McKnight, Third Chorus
7. Scene	Florenceada Gandre and Lee Beardshear
8. Finale	Ensemble
Entr'acte	Orchestra

ACT II.

⁻⁻ Woman's H⁻⁻⁻ ⁻⁻⁻⁻d Chorus

THANX TO "THE POLARIS"

The following article was found in "The Polaris", school paper of North High, Columbus, in a review of the state tourney:

"To Captain Fenner of Day- ton Stivers High goes the dis- tinction of being the best player to compete in the tourney. This little floor guard possessed an uncanny ability of following the ball and was well adent ᵃ rudiments of ᵃ least of

JUNIOR COMMITTEES CHOSEN BY PRESIDEN"

The following junior comm' were appointed by the class pr Paul Ackerman:

Executive committee · Davy, chairman; Dean ma Hollander, Haroᶫ Zartman, Rᵒᵇ man, ᶫ mitᵗ eᵉ

6

Columbus Dispatch 1928

Saturday, April 16, 1932
THE NIAGARA FALLS GAZETTE

Despite Size of War Deficit, Present One Is Bigger Problem

...cratic party leaders in Wash- ...another cow... | The Harding landslide of 1920 left minority member of ...A fights ag... | Cactus Jack, as Garner is familiarly ...ill wears a wide hat... ...he works in hi...

Alfred E. Smith Rose from Poor Boy to Leadership of Party

Alfred E. Smith was born on New York's lower east side on Dec. 30, 1873, almost at the foot of Brooklyn bridge. | He was 13 when his father died.... His mother made umbrellas.... He sold pap... Necessity forced... | On January 15, 1895, he received his first politic... In Janu...

IT'S PRESIDENTIAL YEAR   *Franklin D. Roosevelt*   **Political Headliners**

MELVIN A. TRAYLOR

JOSEPH T. ROBINSON

ALFRED E. SMITH

ALBERT C. RITCHIE

JOHN N. GARNER

FRANKLIN D. ROOSEVELT

GEORGE WHITE

ROBERT J. BULKLEY

These portraits were done as a staff assignment for the New York office of the Associated Press.

1932 Presidential Candidates

HYMN OF HOPE

...CHRISTMAS DAY! —BUT THE WORLD'S IN SUCH A MESS... THERE'S NOT MUCH TO BE JOYFUL ABOUT!

THE YOUNG TERRY SPEAKS AS IF THERE WAS NOTHING TO STRIVE FOR!

GOLLY, DR. PING...IT'S PRETTY BAD!

ONE MAN HAD FAITH IN THE FINAL TRIUMPH OF HUMANITY... LISTEN TO WHAT HE SAID....

" ....FOR NATION SHALL RISE AGAINST NATION, AND KINGDOM AGAINST KINGDOM: THERE SHALL BE FAMINES, AND PESTILENCES, AND EARTHQUAKES IN DIVERS PLACES. ALL THESE ARE THE BEGINNING OF SORROWS.... AND MANY FALSE PROPHETS SHALL RISE, AND SHALL DECEIVE MANY, AND BECAUSE INIQUITY SHALL ABOUND, THE LOVE OF MANY SHALL WAX COLD, BUT HE THAT SHALL ENDURE UNTO THE END, THE SAME SHALL BE SAVED...."

12-25

MILTON CANIFF

'WE WALK BY FAITH, NOT BY SIGHT'

CHRISTMAS EVE! ISN'T IT STRANGE HOW THAT WARM FEELING COMES OVER YOU ON THIS DAY — NO MATTER WHERE YOU ARE?

IT'S NOT PECULIAR TO CHRISTMAS, TERRY... EVERY. RACE OR RELIGION THAT HAS ADVANCED BEYOND BARBARISM HAS AT LEAST ONE DAY SUCH AS THE ONE WE CELEBRATE...

12-24

...IT IS USUALLY THE ANNIVERSARY OF THE BIRTH OF A PERSON WHO IS THE SYMBOL OF THE FAITH OF HIS PEOPLE.... NO MATTER HOW GREAT THE SELFISHNESS AND GREED OF A FEW INDIVIDUALS, MAN HAS A FUNDAMENTAL SENSE OF COMPASSION AND FRATERNITY...

...NO AMOUNT OF PRESSURE CAN CHANGE THE INSTINCTIVE DEVOTION OF PEOPLE TO A PRINCIPLE THEY HAVE CHOSEN TO FOLLOW. MANY LITTLE TYRANTS HAVE TRIED TO SET THEMSELVES UP AS NEW PROPHETS... BUT YOU CAN'T LEGISLATE OR DICTATE A MAN'S SOUL...

A GREAT MANY PEOPLE HAVE DIED, AND ARE DYING, BECAUSE THEY BELIEVED IN THE REASONS FOR A DAY LIKE CHRISTMAS... CONSCIOUSLY OR OTHERWISE, OUR OBSERVANCE OF THE HOLIDAY IS A RENEWAL OF OUR CONVICTION THAT "PEACE ON EARTH, GOOD WILL TOWARD MEN" IS WORTH FIGHTING FOR!.... THOSE DEAD HAVE NOT DIED IN VAIN!

MILTON CANIFF

DRAWING BOARD PATRIOT

by Chris Jenson

It is Christmas, 1947. The worst war the world has ever known has been over for two years. True, there are rumblings in the east, but that's a great distance away . . . nobody cares much. It is a peaceful, prosperous time. If you turn to the comics pages of the nation's newspapers you'll find the various strips are filled with happy holiday messages. The cartoon characters take time out from their daily adventures to join hands around the Christmas tree and wish their readers all the best of the holiday season. Little Orphan Annie, Maggie and Jiggs, even hard-nosed Dick Tracy smiles and says, "I'd say it really is a Merry Christmas."

Near the bottom of the page one strip is very different from the others. The drawing is stark, simple . . . one long panel containing a panoramic view of a lonely, desolate landscape in some faraway place. On the far right stands a simple wooden cross with a soldier's helmet slung from it. In the nighttime sky overhead one star shines out brighter than the rest, illuminating all the world below. There are no smiling cartoon characters here, no pictures of happy children opening presents, no stockings hung from the mantel. There are no Christmas greetings. Like the others, this "comic" strip also has a holiday message, but its message is quite different. Hand lettered across the bottom half of the panel are two paragraphs superimposed on the barren white ground. It begins softly, "Sometimes it's hard to remember how tall he was . . . or how much he weighed. Even with the letters and photographs it's often difficult to make a full, clear picture of what he was like for little questioners who are just now starting to realize that something's missing . . . ."

Reading that strip could raise a lump in the throat of even the most casual reader, but for one who was living it, as many women were on that Christmas Day after the war, the impact could be emotionally devastating, reawakening old memories that were just then beginning to fade. The artist who had created the simple drawing and written the touching sentiment had done so because he had had something to say; partly he wished to express his sympathy and his admiration to those who had lost a loved one in battle, and partly he wanted to remind the more fortunate of the sacrifices others had made in their behalf. Hardly standard holiday fare, this was the Christmas message of Milton Caniff.

The comics are generally perceived as a medium of light entertainment, yet here was a man presenting something which could be intensely personal in nature; it was not a part of some fictional continuing story, and it was certainly not "comic." To understand why Caniff would choose to draw a strip on so important, yet so atypical a theme it is helpful to know something about the man. Born in the heartland of America just as the nation was stepping into its own as a world power, Milton Caniff grew up the all-American boy. The son of an Ohio printer, Caniff was an Eagle Scout who, at a young age, successfully landed jobs with several newspapers. In 1932, after graduating from Ohio State University, he moved to New York to work in the "bullpen" of the Associated Press. While there he created a weekly one panel cartoon feature titled *The Gay Thirties.* He also began *Dickie Dare,* a daily adventure strip aimed at the juvenile market. In 1934 he was approached by the *New York News* to create a new action adventure feature. Caniff's answer was *Terry and the Pirates.* Almost immediately *Terry* took off to widespread critical and public acclaim.

Caniff broke new ground with *Terry.* He introduced subtle, in-depth characterization and realistic, involving plots. His characters were believable, they spoke in mature, witty dialogue and were capable of

artwork began to undergo a gradual evolution, settling finally on something strikingly new and different for the comics. By the 1940s he had developed a classic heavily shadowed style that was to set the tone for all adventure strips to come. Caniff pioneered a drawing style and narrative form that have made him justly famous in and out of his profession.

Aside from the brilliant art and dramatic storyline, one aspect that made *Terry* stand out was Caniff's willingness to deal with, and take a stand on the major issue of the day — fascist expansionism. More than four years before Pearl Harbor, Caniff depicted his characters fighting the Japanese.

As the post-war era began, Caniff left *Terry* and created a new strip, *Steve Canyon;* just as *Terry* was an accurate reflection of its time, *Canyon* mirrored its own world. Initially the title character was a returning veteran, but by the onset of the Korean War, Canyon had reenlisted. There are several reasons why Caniff would put Canyon back in the uniform of his country, but perhaps the most important is that he holds the military in highest regard. "Let's face it, I'm just an out and out patriot," he admits readily. Both his father and grandfather served in the armed forces of the United States in a time of war. "This I'm sure rubbed off on me, because all my life I can remember having the feeling about the individual obligation of a

demonstrating a wide variety of emotions. His settings and props were always fascinatingly authentic. The artwork too was something new for the funny papers. After an initial period throughout *Dickie Dare* and the early *Terry* when Caniff had worked primarily in the light, cartoony style that was popular in the day, his

TERRY AND THE PIRATES by MILTON CANIFF

LET'S TAKE A WALK, TERRY...

YES, SIR, COLONEL CORKIN!

I'M GOING TO MAKE A SPEECH—AND IT'LL BE THE LAST ONE OF ITS KIND IN CAPTIVITY—SO DON'T GET A SHORT CIRCUIT BETWEEN THE EARS...

NO, SIR

WELL, YOU MADE IT...YOU'RE A FLIGHT OFFICER IN THE AIR FORCES OF THE ARMY OF THE UNITED STATES...THOSE WINGS ARE LIKE A NEON LIGHT ON YOUR CHEST...I'M NOT GOING TO WAVE THE FLAG AT YOU—BUT SOME THINGS YOU MUST NEVER FORGET...

...EVERY COUNTRY HAS HAD A HAND IN THE DEVELOPMENT OF THE AIRPLANE—BUT, AFTER ALL, THE WRIGHT BROTHERS WERE A COUPLE OF DAYTON, OHIO, BOYS—AND KITTY HAWK IS STRICTLY IN NORTH CAROLINA... THE HALLMARK OF THE UNITED STATES IS ON EVERY AIRCRAFT...

...SO YOU FIND YOURSELF IN A POSITION TO DEFEND THE COUNTRY THAT GAVE YOU THE WEAPON WITH WHICH TO DO IT... BUT IT WASN'T JUST YOU WHO EARNED THOSE WINGS... A GHOSTLY ECHELON OF GOOD GUYS FLEW THEIR HEARTS OUT IN OLD KITES TO GIVE YOU THE KNOW-HOW...

...AND SOME SMART SLIDE RULE JOKERS SWEAT IT OUT OVER DRAWING BOARDS TO GIVE YOU A MACHINE THAT WILL KEEP YOU UP THERE SHOOTING ... I RECOMMENDED YOU FOR FIGHTER AIRCRAFT AND I WANT YOU TO BE COCKY AND SMART AND PROUD OF BEING A BUZZ-BOY...

...BUT DON'T FORGET THAT EVERY BULLET YOU SHOOT, EVERY GALLON OF GAS AND OIL YOU BURN WAS BROUGHT HERE BY TRANSPORT PILOTS WHO FLEW IT IN OVER THE WORST TERRAIN IN THE WORLD! YOU MAY GET THE GLORY—BUT THEY PUT THE LIFT IN YOUR BALLOON!...

...AND DON'T LET ME EVER CATCH YOU BEING HIGH-BICYCLE WITH THE ENLISTED MEN IN YOUR GROUND CREW! WITHOUT THEM YOU'D NEVER GET TEN FEET OFF THE GROUND! EVERY GREASE MONKEY IN THAT GANG IS RIGHT BESIDE YOU IN THE COCKPIT— AND THEIR HANDS ARE ON THAT STICK, JUST THE SAME AS YOURS...

...YOU'LL GET ANGRY AS THE DEVIL AT THE ARMY AND ITS SO-CALLED RED TAPE...BUT BE PATIENT WITH IT... SOMEHOW, THE OLD EAGLE HAS MANAGED TO END UP IN POSSESSION OF THE BALL IN EVERY WAR SINCE 1776 — SO JUST HUMOR IT ALONG...

14th AIR FORCE U.S.A.F

OKAY, SPORT, END OF SPEECH...WHEN YOU GET UP IN THAT "WILD BLUE YONDER "THE SONG TALKS ABOUT— REMEMBER, THERE ARE A LOT OF GOOD GUYS MISSING FROM MESS TABLES IN THE SOUTH PACIFIC, ALASKA, AFRICA, BRITAIN, ASIA AND BACK HOME WHO ARE SORTA COUNTING ON YOU TO TAKE IT FROM HERE! GOOD NIGHT, KID!

10-17

This way to TOKIO!

Next stop U.S.A.

This page was read into the Congressional record.

WHITE CHRISTMAS—HIMALAYAS VERSION ... QUITE BEAUTIFUL—EXCEPT FOR THE ZEROS AND ROCKS IN THE CLOUDS... AND THE DOWN DRAFTS... BUT THE RIGHT GUYS WHO PUSH OUR STUFF OVER THE HUMP TO CHINA WOULDN'T WANT TO WORRY YOU ON YOUR HOLIDAY... THAT'S WHY THEY RISK IT... SO YOU CAN LOOK AT THE AMERICAN SKY AND SEE NOTHING MORE DANGEROUS THAN SNOW.....

person to bear arms for their country." This opinion, as well as several others of similar patriotic natures surface again and again throughout the collection of strips Caniff designed as Christmas messages to the readers of *Terry* and *Steve Canyon.*

The practice of doing a special strip celebrating Christmas was well established by many cartoonists before Caniff came along. Readers enjoyed seeing their favorite characters in a holiday setting. However, for an adventure strip with a continuing storyline, Christmas poses a unique dilemma. This is because some papers do not print a Christmas Day edition. This causes their readers to miss a day's episode of the story. Caniff began to ponder various solutions. He explains, "In the beginning it was almost a mechanical reason for coming up with something other than the continuity. The point was to do something strong enough and worthwhile enough that the reader would want to read it for itself alone. Even though he might be avidly interested in the continuity

he'd stand still for the one-shot thing. I wanted to do one that was really memorable."

Caniff notes, "I get letters from people saying, 'I look forward again to reading your Christmas strip,' and the person may or may not be a reader or subscriber." While some of the pieces have aged with time, others are just as current as they were when they first appeared. They stand as vignettes of history, each strip the product of a particular point in time, each capturing its own dramatic moment and reflecting the circumstances and attitudes of that moment in history. When taken collectively they offer a fairly accurate picture of American life and world affairs through the last 50 years. Some are tough, some are lyrical, occasionally they are humorous or even poignant, yet running through them all is one central theme: that of maintained vigilance. Caniff puts it simply, "Stay awake ... that's really the heart of the thing. Because I've watched it happen three times in my own lifetime ... this easy falling off to sleep after what seems to be the end of all wars. Three times."

While quite a few of the holiday strips were done praising the U.S. servicemen and women stationed around the world, a variety of themes and topics has successfully been worked in. Many point up the irony of celebrating a holiday of peace while so much of the globe continues to be consumed by war.

Besides the Christmas strips, Caniff will occasionally break continuity for other reasons. The most consistent of these were the Armed Forces Day strips that ran from 1950 to 1965. The theme throughout these strips is very similar to that expressed on Christmas; that the "good Joes" of the armed forces are ready to lay down their lives for your freedom and that you should not forget that they are. In typical Caniff fashion the topics that the individual strips center on are often right out of the headlines. For 1951 the army fighting in Korea provided the theme. 1953 compares soldiers who have just returned from Korea with flood control workers who have returned from managing to hold

back a rising river. By the early '50s America had entered the Cold War, paranoia was rampant, and the mention of the "tide stopped by inches from flooding the land" was an obvious warning of the "Red Menace" many felt was just over the horizon.

Through the late '50s and early '60s Caniff continued to warn of the necessity for maintaining vigilance against communism. He refers to Khrushchev, the space race, the Cuban missile crisis, and the threat of all out nuclear war. Just as the war in Vietnam began to escalate Caniff ended the Armed Forces Day strips. He was being inundated with requests for special strips from a variety of groups and he felt he was overdoing it. "I was beginning to feel like a propagandist," Caniff remembers; "I was overplaying my hand." Caniff does not fail to mention U.S. involvement in Vietnam in his final Armed Forces Day strip. Characteristically he does not sugar coat the reference. While it may be argued that Caniff advocated U.S. involvement in the war, he did not glamorize it.

Tues., Dec. 25, 1945   Terry— "We Drink To Those Who Gave Their All"

DO YOU REMEMBER DUDE HENNICK? TO GIVE THE NEWER READERS OF THIS STRIP A QUICK FILL-IN:—DUDE WAS A REALLY HOT PILOT WITH WHOM TERRY LEE HAD MANY ADVENTURES BEFORE WE ENTERED THE SHOOTING WAR...IT WAS HE WHO FIRST STEERED TERRY'S INTEREST TOWARD AVIATION...AND WHAT IT MEANS TO ATTEMPT TO SOLVE THE BLUE MYSTERY OF THE SKY.

AS HAS OFTEN BEEN THE CASE IN THIS STRIP, DUDE WAS PATTERNED AFTER A REAL PERSON...HIS LIVING COUNTERPART HAD THE SAME WIDE BUCCANEER-BLACK BROWS, CLOSE-CUT HAIR AND THE SHADED EYES OF THE MEN WHO MUST STARE INTO WEATHER.

LIKE HIS ACTUAL DOUBLE, HENNICK HAD BEEN A U.S. ARMY FIGHTER PILOT WHO RESIGNED HIS COMMISSION TO GO TO CHINA IN THE EARLY DAYS OF THE JAPANESE AGGRESSION AS A CIVILIAN FLIGHT INSTRUCTOR FOR CHINESE AIR CADETS.

THE MODEL FOR DUDE HENNICK WAS CAPT. FRANK HIGGS, A CLASSMATE OF MINE AT OHIO STATE UNIVERSITY... DURING THE BITTER, BARREN WAR YEARS HE FLEW UNARMED CARGO AIRCRAFT OVER THE HUMP INTO CHINA — UNTIL HE WAS KILLED IN A CRASH IN THE HILLS SOUTH OF SHANGHAI...

TODAY YOUR MIND WILL BE ON YOUR PARTICULAR GOOD JOE WHO DIDN'T COME BACK FOR CHRISTMAS... BUT IF YOU LIKED DUDE HENNICK YOU MAY WISH TO SPARE A THOUGHT FOR FRANK HIGGS...DUDE DIED WITH HIM...

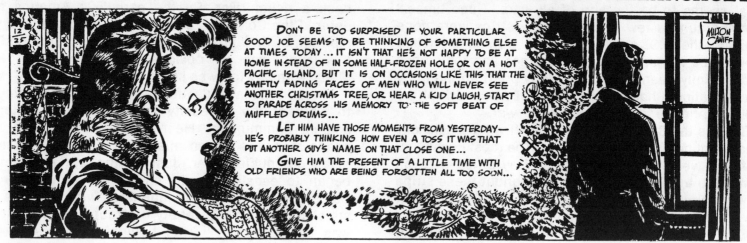

Always pro-American, Caniff will occasionally slip a message espousing love of country into his work. Indeed, the holiday strips are all thinly disguised editorials. Originally Caniff had aspirations of becoming a political cartoonist; some would say he qualifies because of *Terry's* early intervention in the China conflict and *Canyon's* involvement in Korea and Vietnam. Whether that is true or not, certainly the holiday strips would qualify him as such.

Unlike many editorial cartoonists, Caniff does not attack so much as he reminds. Through his brush the medium of the comic strip becomes a combination mirror and magnifying glass, focusing the attention of a too often apathetic American public on matters which it had doubtless taken for granted. Perhaps this is what Caniff does best. He acts as a voice, a teacher, a conscience, making us aware of things we should know about.

Milton Caniff is one of the most famous and successful of all American artists. But he is more than that. During the Second World War no other cartoonist did more for the war effort than Caniff. He devoted many hours of his "spare" time to the preparation of training manuals, pocket guides to foreign countries, bond selling campaigns, and innumerable visits to veterans hospitals. Besides all this he designed seventy different unit insignia and drew *Male Call,* a weekly strip solely for the use of the armed forces. For all of this Caniff never wanted nor received any payment. He did it simply because he felt it was his duty as an American citizen. Over the years he has donated countless drawings to the government as well as to civic and charitable groups, usually for the purpose of bolstering our patriotic spirit and national pride. He has received numerous awards, both civil and military.

For over 50 years Milton Caniff has put his stories, his art, and his point of view in front of the American public on a daily basis. He has been called "the Rembrandt of the comics," "an armchair Marco Polo," and a "genuine creative talent in the field of modern Americana." Yet perhaps the title that fits Milton Caniff best is "drawingboard patriot"; a talented man in love with his country and possessed with a directness of purpose, he is a voice that reminds us of what we are and what we should be. ∎

The Steve Canyon Christmas Strips

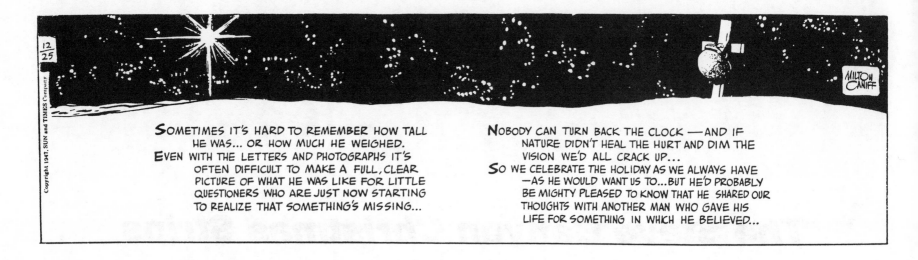

SOMETIMES IT'S HARD TO REMEMBER HOW TALL
HE WAS... OR HOW MUCH HE WEIGHED.
EVEN WITH THE LETTERS AND PHOTOGRAPHS IT'S
OFTEN DIFFICULT TO MAKE A FULL, CLEAR
PICTURE OF WHAT HE WAS LIKE FOR LITTLE
QUESTIONERS WHO ARE JUST NOW STARTING
TO REALIZE THAT SOMETHING'S MISSING...

NOBODY CAN TURN BACK THE CLOCK — AND IF
NATURE DIDN'T HEAL THE HURT AND DIM THE
VISION WE'D ALL CRACK UP...
SO WE CELEBRATE THE HOLIDAY AS WE ALWAYS HAVE
— AS HE WOULD WANT US TO... BUT HE'D PROBABLY
BE MIGHTY PLEASED TO KNOW THAT HE SHARED OUR
THOUGHTS WITH ANOTHER MAN WHO GAVE HIS
LIFE FOR SOMETHING IN WHICH HE BELIEVED...

AFTER EVERY WAR THE VOID IN THE LIVES OF THOSE WHO LOST PERSONAL
LOVED ONES IS DEEP AND TERRIBLE, BUT NATURE IS KINDER TO MAN THAN HE
IS TO HIS FELLOWS, SO THE BITTER EMPTINESS EVOLVES INTO A PERSONAL,
SECRET HURT — PUT AWAY LIKE THE DUSTY DRUMS...

BUT SOME OF THE GOOD JOES DIDN'T GET IT QUICK... THEY STILL LIE ON
COTS OR SIT IN THEIR WHEEL CHAIRS IN VETERANS' HOSPITALS ALL OVER THE
COUNTRY...

THEY'RE NOT BEEFING — THEY KNOW UNCLE SUGAR IS GIVING THEM THE
BEST OF WHAT HE HAS LEARNED OF MEDICINE AND THERAPY, BUT THEY COULD
USE A PASSING THOUGHT FROM YOU FOR WHOM THEY BOUGHT A FREE CHRISTMAS —
THEY PICKED UP THE CHECK FOR YOUR PARTY AND THEY'LL NEVER STOP PAYING
OFF UNTIL THEIR PARTICULAR WAR ENDS...

WE HOPE YOU WON'T FORGET——— THEY CAN'T !

SOMETIMES IT HAPPENS IN A BIG CROWD AT A RAILROAD STATION, OR AT A FOOTBALL GAME ... YOU THINK YOU'VE CONDITIONED YOURSELF, AND THEN YOU HEAR THAT LONG, CLEAR LAUGH— OR A VOICE CALLS OUT HIS FIRST NAME! YOUR BREATH CATCHES IN YOUR THROAT—THEN YOU BRING YOURSELF BACK TO REALITY WITH THE DISCIPLINE ACQUIRED OVER THE EMPTY YEARS ...

WAS IT ALWAYS LIKE THIS? DID PEOPLE HAVE SIMILAR EXPERIENCES AFTER THE REVOLUTIONARY WAR? DID IT HAPPEN WHEN THE NORTH AND SOUTH STOPPED FIGHTING?

...WAS IT THE SAME FOR ALL THAT TIME FROM NOV. 11, 1918, TO DEC. 7, 1941?

IT MUST HAVE BEEN JUST AS HARD TO BELIEVE THAT OFFICIAL NOTIFICATION THEN AS NOW, BUT THAT'S HISTORY— AND THIS IS 1949...FOLKS SAID IT WOULD HURT LESS AND LESS AS THE ACTIVE MEMORY FADED, BUT WHEN THE TREE IS STANDING IN THE FAMILIAR PLACE IT BRINGS BACK EACH HAPPY CHRISTMAS YOU HAD UNTIL YOUR LUCK RAN OUT..

DOING SOMETHING NICE FOR THE GOOD JOES IN THE VETERANS' HOSPITALS EASES THE HURT A LITTLE...THEY'VE HAD A LONG, LONG TOUR—AND NO REPLACEMENTS COMING UP..

MILTON CANIFF

"YOU GET SUCH A DIFFERENT PICTURE OF THINGS FROM THE BUSINESS SIDE OF A HOSPITAL WALL...THERE'S NOT MUCH TALK ABOUT WHY THE GOVERNMENT DID THIS, OR HOW COME THE BIG BRASS DIDN'T DO THAT...

"WE FIGURE WE'RE LUCKY TO HAVE BEEN EVACUATED FROM A STINKING RICE PADDY TO A CLEAN BED IN A STATESIDE HOSPITAL—AND WE'RE GRATEFUL FOR THE INGENUITY AND SKILL THAT SAVED OUR NECKS...

"CONSIDERING ALL THE ODDS, WE CAME OUT AHEAD...NOBODY WANTS TO BE BUSTED UP, BUT WE BEAT THE PERCENTAGES...

"THERE'S JUST ONE THING WE'D LIKE TO GET STRAIGHT WITH CIVILIANS...

" SOME FOLKS TALK ABOUT KOREA AS IF THE ACTION WERE A GOOD-SIZED RIOT FOUGHT BY PROFESSIONAL SOLDIERS WHO ARE EXPECTED TO TAKE SUCH RISKS...

"WE DIDN'T RESENT PEOPLE BACK HOME LIVING REAL GOOD WHILE WE SLUGGED IT OUT IN THE MUD, BUT OUR FRIENDS WHO STOPPED THE BIG ONE OUT THERE ARE JUST AS DEAD AS IF THEY HAD FALLEN AT TRENTON, VICKSBURG, SAN JUAN HILL, THE ARGONNE OR IWO JIMA...

"WHEN WE LICK THIS THING AND PRESERVE THE RIGHT TO MAKE OUR OWN DECISIONS INSTEAD OF GETTING THE ANSWERS OUT OF A DICTATOR'S RULE BOOK, REMEMBER THAT THOSE GOOD JOES BURIED IN FROZEN KOREAN SOIL PAID ONE MORE INSTALLMENT ON <u>YOUR</u> FREEDOM!"

MILTON CANIFF

SIT STILL—WE'LL MAKE IT ALL RIGHT...WE JUST CAME TO ASK A COUPLE OF QUESTIONS...

WE KNOW OUR OWN FOLKS AND CLOSE FRIENDS WORRY ABOUT US AND GIVE A HOOT WHETHER WE SIDESTEP THE PERCENTAGES, BUT WE DON'T QUITE KNOW HOW TO FIGURE SOME OF YOU OTHER CIVILIANS...

OUR SITUATION TODAY IS LIKE WHEN A BIG FIRE BREAKS OUT IN A SMALL TOWN...NOBODY ASKS HOW IT STARTED...THE YOUNG AND ABLE GUYS, AND A FEW OLDER ONES WITH EXPERIENCE, PITCH IN AND FIGHT THE BLAZE SO IT WON'T SPREAD....

THERE'S A FIRE GOING IN THE WORLD RIGHT NOW AND WE HAPPEN TO BE THE AGE GROUP THAT GOT THE NOD TO ANSWER THE ALARM...OKAY— THAT'S THE WAY IT GOES...

WE'LL SMOTHER THIS THING, AND DO A GOOD JOB OF IT, TOO—BUT SOMETIMES WE LOOK AROUND— AND IT'S AS IF NOBODY'S EVEN WATCHING US WORK! —YET THE FLAMES ARE SHOOTING IN EVERY DIRECTION...

LOOK, CITIZEN, WE DON'T MIND OUR NUMBER COMING UP TO CARRY THE HOSE, BUT IT'S YOUR HOUSE WE'RE KEEPING FROM CATCHING FIRE...

G.T. - XXX

PEOPLE OFTEN ASK HOW A CARTOON CAN HAVE AN AIR OF REALITY ABOUT FAR PLACES WHEN THE AUTHOR-ARTIST MUST STAY AT HIS DESK TO KEEP THE STORY MOVING...ONE SOURCE OF INFORMATION IS A GROUP OF FRIENDS WHO WORK IN DISTANT SPOTS AND ARE KIND ENOUGH TO KEEP IN TOUCH...

GEORGE TUCKER, A WAR CORRESPONDENT, DID THIS FOR ME DURING THE BIG SHOW AND AFTERWARD...A TEXAN, COME NORTH BY WAY OF VIRGINIA AND MR. JEFFERSON'S UNIVERSITY, TUCKER STUDIED FIGHTING THROUGH EVERY WORD EVER PUT DOWN ON THE STRUGGLE FOR SOUTHERN INDEPENDENCE. HE WAS READY TO GO ON DEC. 8, 1941....

THE ARMY SAID HIS BLOOD PRESSURE WAS TOO HIGH— SO HE SAW THE CONFLICT WITH A WRITER'S EYES—INEVITABLY MORE THAN ANY SOLDIER EVER COULD HAVE WITNESSED...AN AIRPLANE CRASH AND A NAZI BOMB AT ANZIO TAUGHT HIM WHAT THE BOOKS COULD NOT—AND HE SHARED IT ALL WITH ME ON COUNTLESS TALK-FILLED NIGHTS AFTER PEACE WAS WON.

BUT MARS IS PATIENT...CAME A TIME WHEN OLD HURTS, HALF FORGOTTEN, THROBBED AGAIN AND TOOK THEIR TOLL— FAR FROM THE BILLETS SHARED WITH PYLE AND ALL THE MOTLEY SOLDIERY HE'D KNOWN... THOUGH NOW THE SHEETS WERE CLEAN—AS WELL BECOMES A VICTOR...

SO OFTEN BEFORE HE WAS AWAY AT CHRISTMAS...I'LL TRY TO THINK HE'S ON SOME FAR ASSIGNMENT...AND WILL TELL ME ALL ABOUT IT WHEN WE MEET AGAIN——

12/25

Copyright 1953, Field Enterprises, Inc. Registered U.S. Patent Office.

US — BEEFIN' BECAUSE WE'RE IN THE HOSPITAL ON CHRISTMAS DAY?... YOU MUST BE KIDDIN'!.. MOST OF US WERE UP TO THERE IN KOREAN MUD THIS TIME LAST YEAR — AND SOME OF THE GUYS WERE IN P.O.W. CAMPS WONDERING IF THEY'D SEE TOMORROW MORNING, MUCH LESS A STATESIDE BED WITH CLEAN SHEETS...

WE EVEN GET THAT HERO ROUTINE SOMETIMES —AND WE LET ON LIKE WE THINK IT'S SO MUCH GUFF, BUT DOWN INSIDE WE LIKE IT PLENTY!... THERE'S ONE THING AROUND HERE THOUGH — AND YOU CAN'T HELP NOTICING IT! US KOREA TYPES GET TOGETHER AND YAK IT UP PRETTY GOOD, BUT THE WORLD WAR II G.I.'s, NOT SO MUCH...

THE FELLAHS FROM THE 1918 WAR HARDLY EVEN BOTHER TO BUNCH UP — AND THE SPANISH WAR VETS ARE USUALLY TOO TIRED TO DO MUCH OF ANYTHING...

WHAT? YOU DIDN'T KNOW THERE WERE GUYS FROM THOSE OLD WARS IN THE VETERANS HOSPITALS?.. YEAH... I GUESS SOME OF THEM HAVE OUTLIVED EVEN THEIR KIN — AT LEAST NOBODY EVER COMES TO VISIT THEM! —YOU NOTICE THAT 'SPECIALLY AROUND CHRISTMAS, I GUESS.

...... AS I WAS SAYING — US KOREA GUYS ARE REAL GLAD TO BE IN SUCH A NICE PLACE... BUT NOW AN' THEN WE DO WONDER ABOUT THOSE MEN IN THE FADED BATHROBES...

12/25

Copyright 1954, Field Enterprises, Inc. Registered U.S. Patent Office.

EARLIER THIS MONTH THE OVERSEAS PRESS CLUB OF AMERICA DEDICATED A MEMORIAL PRESS CENTER IN NEW YORK TO THE 80 CORRESPONDENTS WHO HAVE DIED IN FOREIGN LANDS...

WE ARE THE BEST-INFORMED PEOPLE IN THE WORLD TODAY, BUT EVEN THE MEN AND WOMEN WHO GATHER THE NEWS WHICH KEEPS US SO DO NOT EXPECT A BIG DEAL TO BE MADE ABOUT HOW THEY RISK THEIR LIVES ALONG WITH COMBAT SOLDIERS. THEY DRAW CIVILIAN PAY — AND NOBODY DRAFTED THEM... THEY DO NOT SEEK OR ANTICIPATE THE ACCOLADES THAT ARE THE DUE OF MILITARY MEN.

BUT WE THE LIVING REMEMBER THOSE 80 BEYOND BYLINES AND REPORTING AWARDS... THEY WERE OUR FRIENDS — COMPLETE WITH ALL SHADINGS OF APPEARANCE AND OPINION... FROM THE MAN WITH THE WHIPLASH STYLE WHO WOULDN'T BELIEVE A BULLET COULD EVER HAVE HIS NAME ON IT — TO THE MELANCHOLY ONE WHO SOUGHT WAR AND ACCEPTED DEATH AS A SUBSTITUTE FOR AN UNBEARABLE SITUATION IN HIS OWN HOUSE STATESIDE.

THESE WERE OUR PEOPLE — AND THEIR DYING IS A PART OF THE TRADITION OF OUR RIGHT TO SAY, TO READ AND TO HEAR WHAT WE CHOOSE... THEY KNEW THE PRICE OF FREEDOM... THEY PAID IT — TO THE LAST FULL MEASURE... THAT YOU AT HOME MIGHT NEVER WEAR THE SLAVE-CHAINS OF IGNORANCE ....

CITIZEN, DO YOU KNOW WHAT THIS DEVICE SIGNIFIES? IT IS THE SYMBOL OF THE AMERICAN BATTLE MONUMENTS COMMISSION...

DOES IT SEEM A LITTLE OUT OF PLACE TO TALK ABOUT MEMORIALS DURING THE HOLIDAY SEASON?... NOT TO PEOPLE WHO SENT A LOVED ONE OFF TO WAR AND NEVER GOT HIM BACK TO CELEBRATE THIS OR ANY OTHER CHRISTMAS...

THEY KNOW THAT ON THE HALLOWED GROUND WHERE THEIR PARTICULAR HEART LIES BURIED THERE WILL BE PROPER CEREMONIES TO MARK THE OCCASION — AND THAT AT LEAST ONE AMERICAN EX-SERVICE MAN WILL BE ON HAND TO KEEP THE WATCH EVERY DAY!

NONE OF THIS HAPPENS BY ACCIDENT. ...MANY UNSELFISH PEOPLE SPEND TIME AND EFFORT TO SEE THAT OUR DEAD REST IN PEACE AND DIGNITY IN THE LANDS WHERE THEY FOUGHT AND DIED SO THAT WE AT HOME WOULD NOT HEAR A SINGLE SHOT FIRED IN ANGER...

THESE MEN WOULD NOT HAVE WISHED TO DIM YOUR CHRISTMAS WITH SOMBRE THOUGHTS! — THEY WANTED YOU TO BE HAPPY AND FREE FROM FEAR...

...AND WASN'T THAT THE MISSION OF A CERTAIN OTHER PERSON WHO PERISHED VIOLENTLY ON A MOUNTAINSIDE LONG AGO — FAR FROM THE TOWN OF HIS BIRTH?...

MILTON CANIFF

MILTON CANIFF

..... CITIZEN, REMEMBER HOW GOOD YOU FELT? IT WAS CHRISTMAS OF 1946, AND THE WAR HAD BEEN OVER FOR MORE THAN A YEAR... MOST PRICE AND WAGE CONTROLS WERE OFF, AND IT FELT FINE TO MOVE AROUND IN A PEACEFUL WORLD...

THERE WAS ONLY ONE DISTANT, DARK CLOUD... THE FRENCH WERE FIGHTING THE REDS IN INDO-CHINA! WELL-L-L, THAT PART OF THE WORLD SEEMED MIGHTY FAR AWAY, AND BESIDES, WE WEREN'T INVOLVED, SO WHY WORRY? THEN CAME KOREA AND A BRAND-NEW CASUALTY LIST...

AND FINALLY THE PATTERN BEGAN TO EMERGE...

FOLLOWING EACH OF THESE VICIOUS LITTLE WARS WE ARE KEPT OFF BALANCE WAITING FOR THE NEXT OUTBREAK, WHILE SPENDING COUNTLESS BILLIONS FOR ARMAMENT THAT IS OBSOLETE BEFORE IT IS USED...

GOOD PEOPLE ARE KILLED AND OTHERS HURT IN THESE OFF-BEAT ENGAGEMENTS — AND THE SICK ONES WILL GROW LONELY IN THE HOSPITALS.... JUST AS TOO MANY DISABLED MEN FROM OUR FULL-SCALE CONFLICTS WAIT OUT THE DREARY DAYS AND ENDLESS NIGHTS....

YOU COULD DO YOURSELF A FAVOR BY VISITING A VETERANS HOSPITAL AND LETTING THE PATIENTS KNOW YOUR GRATITUDE DID NOT STOP WHEN THE SURRENDER WAS SIGNED —

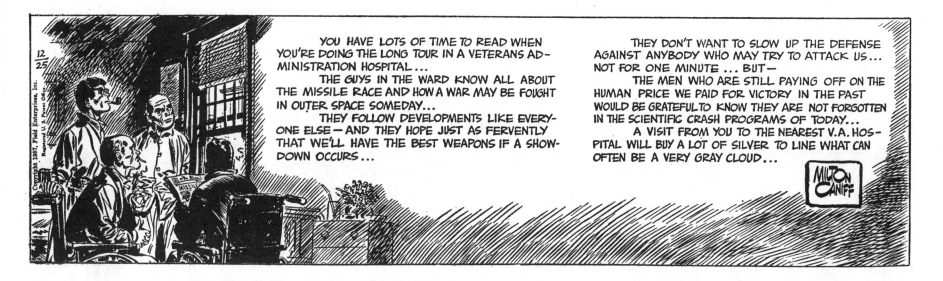

DISTANT CHRISTMAS

WHAT'S THE PERCENTAGE, YOU WHO WALK THE LONELY TOURS
OR STAND THE ICY WATCHES ON THIS CHRISTMAS DAY?
WHY MUST IT BE <u>YOU</u> WHO GETS THE FROZEN HAND OR BLISTERED
FOOT—WHILE OTHERS SIT, WARM AND RELAXED AND
IN COMPANY OF THEIR OWN CHOOSING?

THE REASONS ARE WRITTEN LARGE UPON THE TROUBLED MAP
OF AN EVER-SHRINKING WORLD.

NATIONS WHICH LONG AGO DECKED THEMSELVES WITH HAPPIEST
YULETIDE COLORS ARE NOW ONE MONOTONOUS SHADE OF RED,
WITHOUT IDENTITY EXCEPT AS PART OF A FACELESS UNION
DEDICATED TO THE GRINDING ASSIMILATION OF ALL ABOUT IT.

HOW SHALL WE EVER KNOW THE NUMBER OF SARAJEVOS, THE PEARL
HARBORS, THE KOREAS THAT HAVE BEEN PREVENTED
BY THE MIGHTY HOST OF SUCH LONELY MEN AS YOU, TOO MANY MILES
FROM ALL PRECIOUS THINGS AT THIS HOLY TIME;
YET DOING THE ONE TASK YOUR INSTINCT AND TRAINING TELLS
YOU IS RIGHT... TO PROTECT YOUR LAND
FROM AS FAR AFIELD AS POSSIBLE, IN ORDER NOT TO INVOLVE YOUR
LOVED ONES IN THE CONFLICT?

MAN CAN ENDURE WRACKING TORTURES IF HE HAS HOPE. JUST AS
THIS DAY IS A SYMBOL TO GREAT MASSES OF DEVOUT CHRISTIANS,
SO IS THE AMERICAN FLAG AND UNIFORM A BEACON OF FRIENDSHIP TO
MILLIONS, NOW SILENT,
WHO TAKE STRENGTH FROM YOUR PRESENCE—NEARER TO THEM
THAN TO THE HOMELAND YOU HOLD SO DEAR...

MILTON CANIFF

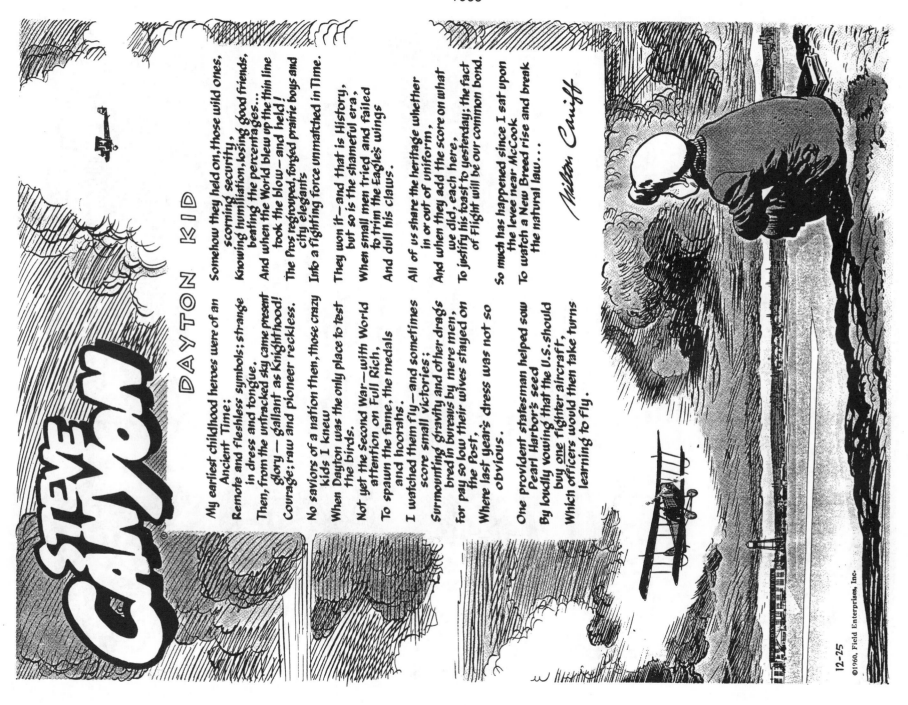

STEVE CANYON

DAYTON KID

My earliest childhood heroes were of an
Ancient Time;
Remote and fleshless symbols; strange
in dress and tongue.
Then, from the untracked sky came present
glory — gallant as Knighthood!
Courage; raw and pioneer reckless.

No saviors of a nation then, those crazy
kids I knew
When Dayton was the only place to test
the birds.
Not yet the Second War — with World
attention on Full Rich,
To spawn the fame, the medals
and hoorahs.

I watched them fly — and sometimes
score small victories;
Surmounting gravity and other drags
bred in bureaus by mere men,
for pay so low their wives stayed on
the Post,
Where last year's dress was not so
obvious.

One provident statesman helped saw
Pearl Harbor's seed
By loudly vowing that the U.S. should
buy one fighter aircraft,
Which officers would then take turns
learning to Fly.

Somehow they held on, those wild ones,
scorning security,
Knowing humiliation, losing good friends,
beating the percentages...
And when the World blew up the thin line
took the blow — and held!
The Pros regrouped, forged prairie boys and
city elegants
Into a fighting force unmatched in Time.

They won it — and that is History,
but so is the shameful era,
When small men tried and failed
to trim the Eagle's wings
And dull his claws.

All of us share the heritage whether
in or out of uniform,
And when they add the score on what
we did, each here,
To justify his toast to yesterday; the fact
of Flight will be our common bond.

So much has happened since I sat upon
the levee near McCook
To watch a New Breed rise and break
the natural law...

Milton Caniff

12-25
©1960, Field Enterprises, Inc.

STEVE CANYON

Since ANNO DOMINI first became the
    Sacred Sign
By which we marked the passing of
    the years,
Men have stood at arms on oh so many
    Christmas Eves,
Far, far from home and warmth of heart
    and hearth.
Bravely they sought the right to form a
    new and independent state,
Or draw a line between two alien ways
    of national life;
But since the guardian miles have shrunk
    in time with engine's beat,
Ambitious men have viewed the fruits of
    freedom with acquisitive eyes...
Unwilling, they, to gain by open toil and
    fair exchange;
The bully instinct rises — and the girded
    fist opens to grasp a neighbors land
And break his will.

So we keep the watch throughout this
    fateful hour
On many fronts around a deeply
    harried globe,
Hopeful that strength of men and
    show of might
Will hold the beasts of ravishment
    at bay...;
Warning against the lust for power which
    breeds the final, fatal ego act of war!

We have come far since that hushed
    desert night
When the faith to which so many
    millions now subscribe
Was bulwarked from the pagan world
    by one lone newborn child.

To those who hold the ramparts of our
    heritage
We bow in gratitude — and hope that
    some not distant Yuletide dawn
Will break — and find good will toward
    other men
In hearts where anger now abides.

MILTON CANIFF

12-24

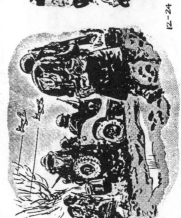

YOU THOUGHT THAT WIRE FROM WASHINGTON WOULD END THE CHRISTMAS RITUAL FOR ALL TIME, BUT CHILDREN DO NOT UNDERSTAND SUCH THINGS—AND SO YOU CARRIED ON...

TWENTY ENDLESS YEARS HAVE PASSED SINCE THAT LAST HURRIED KISS AND WAVE OF HAND, WHICH STOPPED THE CLOCK. SOMETIMES, AS NOW, YOU'RE STARTLED BY HOW MUCH THE BOY LOOKS LIKE THE MAN WHO WALKED THAT VERY PATH ON SUCH A DAY — AND NEVER MADE IT BACK.

YOU'RE PRETTY GOOD AT KEEPING UP A COMPANY FACE UNTIL SOME WISP OF SONG OR HALF-FORGOTTEN PHRASE UNLOCKS OLD DREAMS...

IT'S THEN THAT PHOTOGRAPHS ALREADY TURNING BROWN BECOME AGAIN THE ACTUAL MOMENT AT THE PICNIC OR THE JUNIOR PROM...

THE LETTERS IN THE FADED INK SPRING TO CRISP NEWNESS, TORN IN YOUR HASTE TO GULP THE PRECIOUS WORDS...

BUT NOW YOU PUT YOUR THOUGHTS AWAY AS IF THEY, TOO, WERE SOUVENIRS. THE KIDS WILL SOON RETURN WITH CHRISTMAS DINNER GUESTS...

THEY WILL NOT SEE THE OTHER SMILING FACE THAT BEAMS APPROVAL FROM THE EMPTY CHAIR...

Milton Caniff

THERE ARE GOOD MEN BEING KILLED IN BRUSH-FIRE WARS IN PLACES YOU CAN'T EVEN SPELL OR PRONOUNCE...

AND TWO-BIT DICTATORS ARE YAPPING AT OUR HEELS FROM SEVERAL COUNTRIES AROUND THE RESTLESS EDGES OF A SEETHING WORLD...

SO SOMETIMES YOU FEEL FRUSTRATED AND ANGRY BECAUSE SOMETHING ISN'T BEING DONE TO SLAP DOWN THE WHINING INSECTS OF INTERNATIONAL POLITICS...

WELL, SOMETHING IS BEING ACCOMPLISHED!

MANY MORE 'KIDS NEXT DOOR' ARE STANDING ON FAR BORDERS — WHERE THEIR VERY PRESENCE IS KEEPING SOME CHARACTER FROM SHOWING OFF TO GRAB PUBLICITY AND ADDITIONAL FOREIGN AID MONEY.

GIVE A THOUGHT TO THIS NEW BREED WHEN YOU EAT THAT CHRISTMAS DINNER — AND ADD A WORD OR TWO WHEN YOU SAY GRACE —FOR THE OTHER NICE GUYS WHO NEVER MADE IT HOME FROM THE VETERANS' HOSPITALS...

THEY BOUGHT YOU THAT PEACEFUL MEAL WITH THE CURRENCY OF TIME, WHICH CAN NEVER BE RE-PAID, EXCEPT WITH GRATITUDE!

MILTON CANIFF

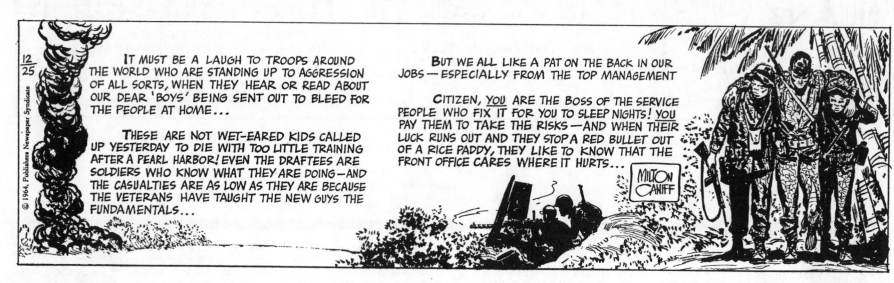

12/25

© 1964, Publishers Newspaper Syndicate

IT MUST BE A LAUGH TO TROOPS AROUND THE WORLD WHO ARE STANDING UP TO AGGRESSION OF ALL SORTS, WHEN THEY HEAR OR READ ABOUT OUR DEAR 'BOYS' BEING SENT OUT TO BLEED FOR THE PEOPLE AT HOME...

THESE ARE NOT WET-EARED KIDS CALLED UP YESTERDAY TO DIE WITH TOO LITTLE TRAINING AFTER A PEARL HARBOR! EVEN THE DRAFTEES ARE SOLDIERS WHO KNOW WHAT THEY ARE DOING—AND THE CASUALTIES ARE AS LOW AS THEY ARE BECAUSE THE VETERANS HAVE TAUGHT THE NEW GUYS THE FUNDAMENTALS...

BUT WE ALL LIKE A PAT ON THE BACK IN OUR JOBS—ESPECIALLY FROM THE TOP MANAGEMENT

CITIZEN, YOU ARE THE BOSS OF THE SERVICE PEOPLE WHO FIX IT FOR YOU TO SLEEP NIGHTS! YOU PAY THEM TO TAKE THE RISKS—AND WHEN THEIR LUCK RUNS OUT AND THEY STOP A RED BULLET OUT OF A RICE PADDY, THEY LIKE TO KNOW THAT THE FRONT OFFICE CARES WHERE IT HURTS...

MILTON CANIFF

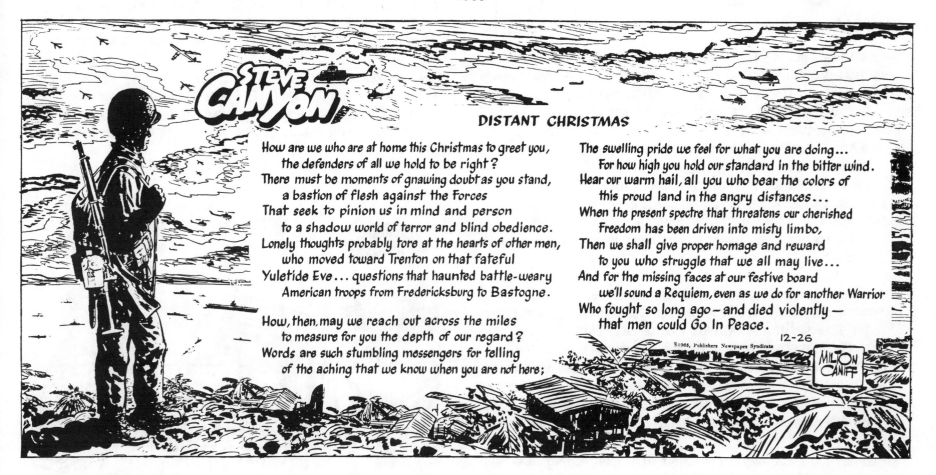

DISTANT CHRISTMAS

How are we who are at home this Christmas to greet you,
    the defenders of all we hold to be right?
There must be moments of gnawing doubt as you stand,
    a bastion of flesh against the Forces
That seek to pinion us in mind and person
    to a shadow world of terror and blind obedience.
Lonely thoughts probably tore at the hearts of other men,
    who moved toward Trenton on that fateful
Yuletide Eve... questions that haunted battle-weary
    American troops from Fredericksburg to Bastogne.

How, then, may we reach out across the miles
    to measure for you the depth of our regard?
Words are such stumbling messengers for telling
    of the aching that we know when you are not here;

The swelling pride we feel for what you are doing...
    For how high you hold our standard in the bitter wind.
Hear our warm hail, all you who bear the colors of
    this proud land in the angry distances...
When the present spectre that threatens our cherished
    Freedom has been driven into misty limbo,
Then we shall give proper homage and reward
    to you who struggle that we all may live...
And for the missing faces at our festive board
    we'll sound a Requiem, even as we do for another Warrior
Who fought so long ago — and died violently —
    that men could Go In Peace.

12-26

© 1965, Publishers Newspaper Syndicate

CHRISTMAS CARD TO A LONELY LADY

WHY HAS THIS BLOW STRUCK AT <u>YOU</u> IN THE FIRST FLOWER OF THE
LOVE THAT WAS THE BECKONING GOAL OF ALL THOSE GROWING YEARS?
    WHY, WHEN THE WINE OF SWEET FULFILLMENT WAS
    BUT AN INITIAL TASTE UPON THE TONGUE?
NOW THE GLOWING PROMISE OF ENDURING YEARS IS TURNED
TO DREAD BY EVERY MOCKING JANGLE OF THE PHONE,
    BECAUSE YOUR MAN HAS GONE — CALLED FROM
    WARM EMBRACE TO DRILL GROUND CHILL!
IT'S ALL SO VAGUE, REMOTE; OF NO CONCERN TO YOU.. A DIRTY,
BLOODY FIGHT IN PLACES WITH THOSE NAMES YOU CAN'T PRONOUNCE...
    BUT IF YOU ARE ALONE — WHAT IS THAT TOUCH UPON YOUR SHOULDER?
    WHO NOW INTRUDES UPON YOUR PRIVATE SORROW PLACE?

WITHIN YOUR OWN LIFE CYCLE THERE ARE THREE FULL GROUPS
OF WOMEN — MUCH LIKE YOU, WHO FACED THE SAME HARSH TURN OF FATE!
    THE TRENCHES OF A BLUDGEONED FRANCE WERE ENDLESS
    WORLDS AWAY FOR HOME FRONT-GIRLS IN NINETEEN-SEVENTEEN,
IN FORTY-ONE A SEAR DECEMBER SUNDAY CHANGED THE LIVES AND FORTUNES
OF A GENERATION, MALE AND FEMALE, FRIEND AND FOE — AND JUST YOUR AGE.
    KOREA CAME BEFORE THE WOUNDS HAD SCARCELY FORMED A SCAR..
    WOMEN AGAIN WERE CALLED UPON TO WAIT AS YOU MUST DO TODAY.

SO, LONELY LADY, YOU ARE NOT IN LIMBO WITH YOUR ACHING HEART.
THE STEEL-SOFT CHAIN OF SHARED DISTRESS IS PRESENT WITH YOU NOW,
    THAT WARMTH CONVEYED FROM OTHERS WHO HAVE KNOWN
    THE AWFUL EMPTINESS THAT DEEPENS AT THIS HOLY HOUR.

12-25

MOST OF THE YOUNG MEN SERVE THEIR TIME, RETURNING WITH
THE SPARK TO LIGHT THE DARKNESS LEFT BY MONTHS AWAY,
    BUT IF YOUR LUCK RUNS OUT, NO MATTER HOW THE PAIN
    PERSISTS — YOU'LL BE FOREVER SPRING TO HIM — AND HE TO YOU.

EVEN AS EVERY IMAGE OF THAT ONE FOR WHOM WE KEEP THIS
DAY APART — IS YOUTH IN FULLEST BLOOM STRUCK DOWN IN ANGER —
    IN SACRIFICE THAT PEOPLE YET UNBORN MIGHT ONE DAY KNOW
    THE PEACE FOR WHICH HE GAVE HIS LIFE BEFORE HIS TIME!

- BITTERNESS BETWEEN OLD FRIENDS...
- PROSPERITY FOR SOME PEOPLE—IN THE FACE OF POVERTY FOR OTHERS...
- HEAVY TAXES...
- RACIAL TENSION...
- JAIL WITHOUT TRIAL
- DISTRUST OF AUTHORITY...
- UNPOPULAR WARS IN FAR PLACES...
- UNSAFE CITY STREETS
- DISDAINFUL CHILDREN
- FRUSTRATED PARENTS
- CRUMBLING OF OLD IDEALS...

1967 HEADLINES? NO INDEED! THIS WAS THE YEAR OF BETHLEHEM—WHEN HOPE WAS BORN FOR GENERATIONS YET TO COME...

YOUNG MEN STOOD AT ARMS THAT STAR-BRIGHT NIGHT—JUST AS THEY DID THIS HOLY EVE JUST PAST...DEFENDING WHAT THEY FELT WAS RIGHT.

FROM DEEP TRAVAIL SO OFTEN COMES THE SWEEP OF LIFTED SPIRIT—THUS, TODAY, PERHAPS WE TOE THE THRESHOLD OF A FINER TIME.

BUT APATHY AND GREED ARE NOT THE TOOLS FOR BRINGING PEACE TO TROUBLED HEARTS AND MINDS.

THE MANGER CHILD GREW UP TO MARTYR'S FATE, YET LEFT A TEXT THAT OFFERS STRENGTH TO JUSTIFY OUR OWN BRIEF MOMENT IN THE SUN...

MILTON CANIFF

1968

LOOK, CITIZEN...

FOR THE MOMENT FORGET ABOUT HAWKS AND DOVES; THE SHOULDS AND SHOULD NOTS...

WHEN A QUARTER OF A MILLION GOOD GUYS ARE OUT IN A PLACE YOU CAN'T PRONOUNCE, DOING A DIRTY JOB, WITH A POTENTIAL BOMB OR SNIPER BULLET AROUND EVERY BEND, WHETHER IT IS A JUNGLE TRAIL OR CITY STREET, THE REALLY BIG ISSUE LIES IN BACKING THEM UP—FOR THE GOOD OF THEIR SOULS... AND YOURS!

LET THE HISTORY BOOKS GO INTO THE GLOBAL ASPECTS AND IMPLICATIONS OF THE VIET-NAM THING...

RIGHT NOW IT IS A MATTER OF HURTING WHEN YOU'RE HIT—AND HOPING TO FIX IT SO THE FOLKS AT HOME NEVER HAVE TO DROP TO THEIR KNEES BEFORE A CHARACTER WEARING A RED STAR...

...BUT FIX IT THERE—INSTEAD OF ON MAIN STREET!

MILTON CANIFF

HEY, CITIZEN=

IN MANY WAYS THIS HAS BEEN A STINKY YEAR...

THE OLD VALUES HAVE TAKEN A BEATING!—ANY THOUGHT INTRODUCED BEFORE LAST TUESDAY COMES UP LABELED "EARLY ANCIENT"!

BUT DON'T PUT THE DISSENTERS DOWN WITHOUT A LISTEN...

WHEN G.W. AND HIS RAGGY-TAILED MOB CROSSED THE DELAWARE 195 YEARS AGO LAST NIGHT THEY WERE TELLING OLD GEORGE THREE ABOUT A NEW STACK OF STANDARDS —

LIKE LIBERTY, MAN! FREE SPEECH! AND ALL THAT TRASH!

WELL, IT STUCK — AND THIS IS THE PLACE, HOLLER-GUY! WHERE YOU MAY YELL 'FOUL' AND LIVE TO DEFEND YOUR POINT! AND IF YOU DON'T LIKE THE BOSS YOU CAN TELL HIM TO FRY HIS HAT—AND WALK OUT...

THERE ARE SOME CHARACTERS IN THE MICKEY MOUSE SUITS OUT THERE RIGHT NOW RISKING THEIR LIVES, LIBERTIES AND THEIR SACRED HONOR TO INSURE <u>YOUR</u> RIGHT TO PEACEFUL SLEEP TONIGHT!

MILTON CANIFF

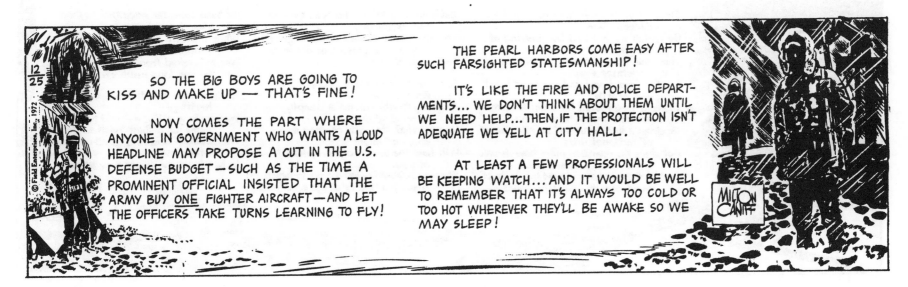

SO THE BIG BOYS ARE GOING TO KISS AND MAKE UP — THAT'S FINE!

NOW COMES THE PART WHERE ANYONE IN GOVERNMENT WHO WANTS A LOUD HEADLINE MAY PROPOSE A CUT IN THE U.S. DEFENSE BUDGET — SUCH AS THE TIME A PROMINENT OFFICIAL INSISTED THAT THE ARMY BUY <u>ONE</u> FIGHTER AIRCRAFT — AND LET THE OFFICERS TAKE TURNS LEARNING TO FLY!

THE PEARL HARBORS COME EASY AFTER SUCH FARSIGHTED STATESMANSHIP!

IT'S LIKE THE FIRE AND POLICE DEPARTMENTS... WE DON'T THINK ABOUT THEM UNTIL WE NEED HELP... THEN, IF THE PROTECTION ISN'T ADEQUATE WE YELL AT CITY HALL.

AT LEAST A FEW PROFESSIONALS WILL BE KEEPING WATCH... AND IT WOULD BE WELL TO REMEMBER THAT IT'S ALWAYS TOO COLD OR TOO HOT WHEREVER THEY'LL BE AWAKE SO WE MAY SLEEP!

MILTON CANIFF

12/25

© Field Enterprises, Inc., 1973

OF COURSE, CITIZEN, YOU MADE BIG, PARTISAN NOISES WHEN THE HOT FIGHTING WAS WORLDS AWAY AND NO ONE LOUSED UP YOUR OWN LOCAL PATTERN OF LIFE...

NOW THEY'RE SEPARATING THE MEN FROM THE CRYBABIES, RIGHT HERE ON MAIN STREET, BUT THE AIR RAIDS COME FROM THE MOUTHS OF PEOPLE INSTEAD OF CANNON!

IT IS KIND OF HARD TO GROW OUT OF OUR POLITICAL PUBERTY...

—BUT REASSURING TO REMEMBER—THAT, EVEN AS WE ARE TRYING TO SHAKE OFF THE GREATEST DOMESTIC HANGOVER SINCE THE CIVIL WAR...

THERE ARE SOME DEDICATED MEN AND WOMEN MINDING THE STORE IN BRANCH OFFICES AROUND THE WORLD...

TOO BAD ALL THE HOME-GROAN, PART-TIME PATRIOTS CAN'T KNOW HOW IT FEELS TO BE IN SOME FAR, ALIEN CITY AND SEE THAT PRETTY THING RUN UP A FLAG— STAFF IN THE DAWN'S EARLY LIGHT...

MAYBE OLD FRANK KEY KNEW WHAT HE WAS TALKING ABOUT!

MILTON CANIFF

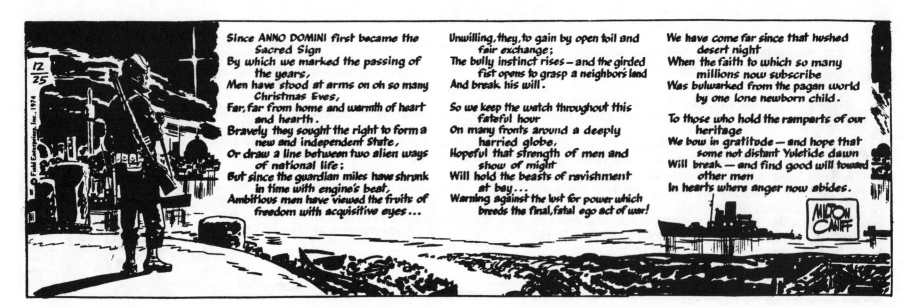

12/25

© Field Enterprises, Inc., 1974

Since ANNO DOMINI first became the Sacred Sign
By which we marked the passing of the years,
Men have stood at arms on oh so many Christmas Eves,
Far, far from home and warmth of heart and hearth.
Bravely they sought the right to form a new and independent State,
Or draw a line between two alien ways of national life;
But since the guardian miles have shrunk in time with engine's beat,
Ambitious men have viewed the fruits of freedom with acquisitive eyes...

Unwilling, they, to gain by open toil and fair exchange;
The bully instinct rises — and the girded fist opens to grasp a neighbor's land
And break his will.

So we keep the watch throughout this fateful hour
On many fronts around a deeply harried globe,
Hopeful that strength of men and show of might
Will hold the beasts of ravishment at bay...
Warning against the lust for power which breeds the final, fatal ego act of war!

We have come far since that hushed desert night
When the faith to which so many millions now subscribe
Was bulwarked from the pagan world by one lone newborn child.

To those who hold the ramparts of our heritage
We bow in gratitude — and hope that some not distant Yuletide dawn
Will break — and find good will toward other men
In hearts where anger now abides.

MILTON CANIFF

12/25

© Field Enterprises, Inc. 1975

HEY, KIDDO, THE DIRTY OLD MILITARY REALLY GOT ITS COMEUPPANCE, DIDN'T IT? THE BABY-BOMBERS AND MONEY-GUZZLING CANOE CLUB SWABBIES WERE CUT DOWN TO SIZE — ALONG WITH THE PX COMMANDOS WHO GOOFED OFF ON OUR TAX-MONEY PAYROLL ... A REAL VICTORY FOR COMMON SENSE!

—— ONLY ONE TROUBLE ...

YOU KEEP READING ABOUT THAT SOVIET NUCLEAR-SUB FLEET ... AND HOW THE REDS HAVE MOVED INTO FORMERLY FRIENDLY FREE COUNTRIES ... AND HOW WE'RE RUNNING EVEN ON MISSILES AND BOMBERS ... AND WHO DOES WHAT, IF IVAN DECIDES WE ARE SOFT ENOUGH ...

THEN YOU THINK OF THAT THIN YANK LINE IN THE ANGRY DISTANCES — AND YOU ARE GRATEFUL FOR THE PROTECTION ... WHILE WE ARE HAVING OUR BOOTY SLEEP!

MILTON CANIFF

1976

12/25

© Field Enterprises, Inc. 1976

HEY! IS THERE SOMETHING WRONG? ANOTHER CHRISTMAS AND NOBODY IS SHOOTING AT US!

MAYBE IT IS LIKE THE OLD YARN ABOUT TWO OPPOSING SENTRIES WHO MET ON PATROL. ONE, WHO WAS PROUD OF HOW SHARP HE KEPT HIS KNIFE, TOOK A WIDE SWING AT HIS ENEMY! "MISSED" HISSED THE SLOWER MAN ON THE DRAW! THE PROUD ONE SAID, "WAIT UNTIL YOU TRY TO SHAKE YOUR HEAD."

POINT IS = YOU WERE CALLED UP FOR KOREA OR VIET NAM. YOU DID YOUR HITCH AND CAME BACK WHOLE! GOT TO SCHOOL ON THE G.I. BILL, NOW MARRIED AND TRYING TO HACK OUT A LIVING, LIKE EVERYONE ELSE ....

BUT ALL THE TIME YOU HEAR WHAT A MISERABLE PEOPLE WE'VE BECOME, THAT THE OLD DREAM HAS FADED; THE GOVERNMENT IS CORRUPT, AND SO ON ....

THEN WE GO TO THE POLLS, CHANGE LEADERSHIP — AND NONE OF THE DEPARTING STAFF ARE PUT IN JAIL OR EXE-CUTED. NO NEWSPAPER OR RADIO-TV STATIONS TAKEN OVER ...

WE'VE BEEN MALIGNED, RIDICULED AND USED BY THE BIG-BROTHER CROWD, BUT IT COMES UP NICE TO KNOW THAT YOU CAN LOOK ANY MAN IN YOUR COUNTRY IN THE EYE AND TELL HIM TO GO TO HELL!

—IT MAKES FOR A MIGHTY SHARP KNIFE — WHEN YOU NEED IT!

MILTON CANIFF

12/26

NO ONE EVER TALKS ABOUT THE DAY <u>AFTER CHRISTMAS</u>! MAYBE IT'S BECAUSE THAT IS THE BIG LETDOWN TIME...THE HANG-OVER AFTER SPENDING ALL THAT MONEY, OR EATING ALL THAT WHITE MEAT.

YET, THIS IS ONE OF THE MOST IM-PORTANT DAYS IN THE HISTORY OF THE UNITED STATES! GENERAL WASHINGTON WAITED UNTIL THE HESSIAN TROOPS AT TREN-TON HAD LIVED IT UP ON CHRISTMAS DAY— <u>THEN</u> HE LET THEM HAVE IT!

THOSE RAGGY—TAILED COLONIALS HAD NO THROBBING HEADS OR OVER-USED CREDIT CARDS....OF COURSE THEY LEFT SOME RED STAINS IN THE SNOW AS THEY CROSSED THE DELAWARE AND HEADED FOR THE SLEEP-ING TOWN...BUT WHAT'S A LITTLE 3 A.M. BARE-FOOT HIKE IN THE ICY SLUSH WHEN YOU'RE ABOUT TO FORM A NATION WHICH WILL BE FREE—TO FORGET THE WHOLE THING.

THE BRITISH DIDN'T FORGET! QUOTE= (FROM THE PARLIAMENTARY RECORD) "ALL OUR HOPES WERE BLASTED BY THAT UNHAPPY AFFAIR AT TRENTON!"

JUST THOUGHT YOU'D LIKE TO KNOW...

MILTON CANIFF

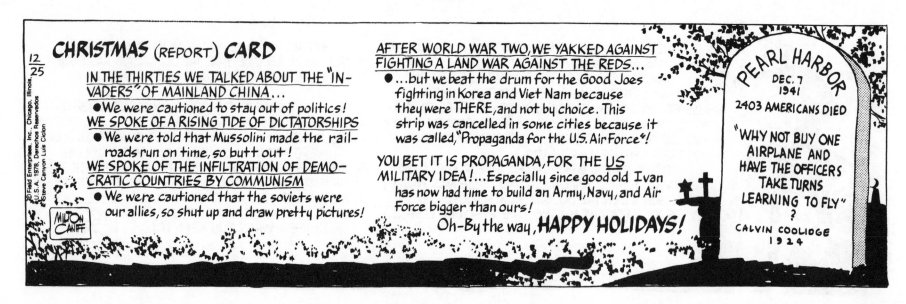

12/25

CHRISTMAS (REPORT) CARD

IN THE THIRTIES WE TALKED ABOUT THE "IN-VADERS" OF MAINLAND CHINA...
- We were cautioned to stay out of politics!

WE SPOKE OF A RISING TIDE OF DICTATORSHIPS
- We were told that Mussolini made the rail-roads run on time, so butt out!

WE SPOKE OF THE INFILTRATION OF DEMO-CRATIC COUNTRIES BY COMMUNISM
- We were cautioned that the soviets were our allies, so shut up and draw pretty pictures!

MILTON CANIFF

AFTER WORLD WAR TWO, WE YAKKED AGAINST FIGHTING A LAND WAR AGAINST THE REDS...
- ...but we beat the drum for the Good Joes fighting in Korea and Viet Nam because they were THERE, and not by choice. This strip was cancelled in some cities because it was called, "Propaganda for the U.S. Air Force"!

YOU BET IT IS PROPAGANDA, FOR THE <u>US</u> MILITARY IDEA!...Especially since good old Ivan has now had time to build an Army, Navy, and Air Force bigger than ours!

Oh-By the way, **HAPPY HOLIDAYS!**

PEARL HARBOR
DEC. 7
1941
2403 AMERICANS DIED

"WHY NOT BUY ONE AIRPLANE AND HAVE THE OFFICERS TAKE TURNS LEARNING TO FLY" ?

CALVIN COOLIDGE 1924

12/25

TEN YEARS AFTER WORLD WAR I, I WAS IN HEIDELBERG, GERMANY. I TURNED A CORNER AND ALMOST BUMPED INTO A GERMAN ARMY OFFICER. I WAS STARTLED BY THIS FACE-TO-FACE ENCOUNTER WITH THE UNIFORM OF THE SO RECENT ENEMY. I HAD THE FEELING THAT THERE WAS MORE TO COME. IT DID!

...NOT LONG AGO I WAS AT THE BRANDENBURG GATE IN WEST BERLIN. THE RUSSIAN GUARD WAS JUST CHANGING, AND I AGAIN GOT THAT SENSE OF THE OMINOUS FROM BEING SO CLOSE TO A POTENTIAL FUTURE OPPONENT.

WHEN SOVIET COMBAT TROOPS MOVED INTO CUBA, I ONCE MORE FELT THAT CHILL OF CONCERN AT AN ALIEN MILITARY PRESENCE SO CLOSE AT HAND.

IF IT WERE NOT FOR THE TOO-THIN RED, WHITE AND BLUE LINE OF YANKEE MEN AND WOMEN ABOUT THE WORLD, WE COULD BE HAVING AN EVEN CLOSER LOOK AT HOSTILE UNIFORMS.

YOU MIGHT GIVE IT SOME THOUGHT WHEN YOU ARE COUNTING YOUR BLESSINGS ON THE BIRTHDAY OF ONE WHO KNEW WHAT IT WAS LIKE TO HAVE RAW HATE CLOSING IN FROM EVERYWHERE — INCLUDING PEOPLE WHO ONCE SAID THEY LOVED HIM.

MILTON CANIFF

WE HAVE BEEN ACCUSED OF WARMONGERING..... SO TO AVOID THAT ONEROUS CONCEPT...

12/25

THIS GENTLE COMMUNICATION IS TO POINT OUT WHAT A FASCINATING VIEW MAY BE HAD BY ANY U.S. SEAMAN STANDING CHRISTMAS DAY WATCH ON A U.S. VESSEL IN THE PERSIAN GULF.

THE PLEASURE CRAFT ARE GATHERED HERE TO ENJOY THE WARM WATERS NOT PRESENT IN THEIR HOME PORTS — AND TO OFFER TOTAL PROTECTION TO GULFSIDE COMMUNITIES, EVEN IF THOSE NATIONS HAVE BEEN SO SHORT-SIGHTED AS TO FAIL TO REQUEST SUCH GENEROUS ABSORPTION.

OH, YES... HAVE A MERRY CHRISTMAS

MILTON CANIFF

12/25

CHRISTMAS STORY
(DELAYED TRANSMISSION)

WHEN I WAS A YOUNG KID IN HILLSBORO, OHIO, LIVING VETERANS OF THE CIVIL WAR WERE STILL AROUND. MY GREAT-GRANDFATHER WAS ONE OF THEM. HE LIVED IN THE COUNTRY, SO THE FAMILY SAW HIM SELDOM, BUT ALWAYS AT CHRISTMAS.

THE OLD MAN WOULD TELL HOW HE HAD ARRIVED IN AMERICA ONE BITE AHEAD OF THE POTATO FAMINE — JUST ABOUT THE TIME OF FORT SUMTER. HE COULD RIDE AND CARE FOR A HORSE, SO HE WAS WELCOMED BY THE FIRST OHIO CAVALRY, SIGNING HIS NAME WITH AN 'X' ON THE ENLISTMENT PAPERS.

AFTER FOUR YEARS AND TWO WOUNDS, HE WAS DISCHARGED, RECEIVING A SMALL CASH PENSION, AUGMENTED BY AN ISSUE OF WHISKEY AND TOBACCO.... HE DRANK THE WHISKEY AND STUFFED THE LEAF INTO A CLAY PIPE, LIGHTING UP WITH A SMALL MAGNIFYING GLASS. WHEN IT WAS. CLOUDY HE CHEWED THE TOBACCO... (MATCHES COST MONEY!)

ON THOSE CHRISTMAS DAY AFTERNOONS, THE OLD SOLDIER WOULD SIT IN FRONT OF THE FIRE, FAVORING HIS CROOKED LEG, CRUSHED BY A HORSE SHOT FROM UNDER HIM. HE OFTEN SPOKE OF THE PRIVILEGE IT HAD BEEN TO FIGHT FOR THIS NEW COUNTRY — WHICH WOULD ALLOW AN ILLITERATE IMMIGRANT LAD TO OWN HIS OWN HOUSE, LAND AND HORSE — AND BE ABLE TO TELL ANY MAN TO GO TO HELL!

12/25

NOEL SICKLES!

YOU MAY NOT RECOGNIZE THE NAME, BUT YOU KNOW HIS WORK... BECAUSE HE WAS IMITATED BY EVERY NEWSPAPER ADVENTURE-STORY CARTOONIST AFTER 1933.

THIS RESTLESS GENIUS WAS THE GREATEST NATURAL ARTIST I EVER KNEW. HE HAD NO FORMAL TRAINING, BUT IN THOSE HIGH SCHOOL YEARS WHEN THE OTHERS OF US WERE CHASING THE GIRLS AND LEARNING THE LATEST DANCE STEP, SICKLES WAS AT THE PUBLIC LIBRARY COPYING THE GREAT ILLUSTRATORS....

WHEN WORLD WAR TWO STARTED, THE PENTAGON PULLED NOEL RIGHT OUT OF THE DRAFT BOARD BECAUSE HE ALREADY KNEW MORE ABOUT AXIS WEAPONS AND EQUIPMENT THAN GENERAL MARSHALL.

NOW HE IS DEAD! — ALL THAT TALENT STILL UNUSED — AND EVERY CARTOONIST FEELS CHEATED OF WHAT MIGHT YET HAVE COME FROM HIS MAGIC HAND.

MY OWN GRIEF GOES EVEN DEEPER, BUT THAT IS A PRIVATE THING.

BACK TO CHILLICOTHE, BUD... BILL IRELAND IS WAITING.

CHRISTMAS CHOW, then and now

Since congress cried `ENOUGH'
    to George the third in Seventy Six,
Americans have stood at arms
    on Christmas Day at some beleaguered post.
Lonely and cold or lonely and hot,
    it is always the wrong place,
However right the reasons in the books.

The agony of Valley Forge,
    and all that went before,
Has dimmed with time and legends;
    fiction filled,
But Yuletide cheer and frozen feet
    cannot be reconciled.
So history records that Washington
    reversed the Hessians' Christmas plans
To raise Colonial hopes from deep despair.

In Mexico, the re-fried beans, tequilla
    and the other vast array,
Killed more invading troops
    than Santa Anna's guns.

Black-eyed peas and turnip greens,
    Sow-belly pork and goober peas
May be evolved into a king's repast—
    when time's a lazy cat—
But with the Yankee guns just down the pike,
    the feast was pone and branch
And don't fall out!

Exotic Cuba in the Spanish War
    was never Grandma's Place for Yuletide Joy
Mosquitoes armed like kamikazes came to lunch
    and left a yellow calling card behind.

Slumgullion was all-purpose name
    for what the cooks could bring to pass
When 'mess' was all too real a word
    for what was slapped on eating gear
As Christmas fare in Seventeen.

The claim is made that sailors have
    a better chance to live it up on Christmas Day.
Which may be fair to say—or not, but all it took
    was one clean hit at water line
And all on board could soon be chewing knuckles
    on a raft, if they got lucky-quick.

C-Rations never made for Christmas cheer
    until you saw them pounced upon
By orphan kids, no matter where you were.
    A stick of chewing gum in grubby hands
Was candy cane—and stocking filled.

The Murmansk Run was just the place for chow
    while standing General Quarters hours on end.
A gun tub's hardly built for carving, hot or cold
    and stuffing leaves the plate
When waves are high.

Python roasted on a jungle flame
    is not the Ritz de Ritz.
But gratitude for being whole
    is condiment enough.

Korean food is famous (in the books),
    but Pork Chop Hill was not the proving place,
And feasting under fire is not digesting at its best
    Plum pudding a la Chinese bugles in the dark
Redlined those Christmas Days forevermore.

When 'Nam was just a travel folder name
    the thought of Yuletide cruises sounded great,
But Spam among the paddies didn't taste like home
    and mortar rounds could wreck the Silent Night.

We reasoned that it _must_ have run its course,
    this urge to rock the global boat each thirty years or so,
But right on time the bully boys are at it once again.
    This year the Yank Marines have felt the blow
Instead of being home with family and friends.

And all this strife short miles from where
    this Birthday came to pass.
He tried to tell us how to love, but
    neighbors seldom heed the reasoned word.

Now we may only hope that his own sacrifice
    will not have been in vain

As now it seems

HEY, CITIZEN =

EVER THINK HOW IT WOULD FEEL THIS CHRISTMAS MORNING TO BE THE YANK MARINE (PROBABLY NOT IN UNIFORM — TO KEEP A LOW NATIONAL PROFILE) WHO FIRST GREETS A CAR WHEN IT DRIVES UP TO THE U.S. EMBASSY IN ANY COUNTRY ? EVEN IN A FRIENDLY NATION THE AUTOMOBILE MAY BE PACKED WITH HIGH EXPLOSIVES TO BE SET OFF BY THE SUICIDE DRIVER.

NOT LIKELY THAT THE GYRENE

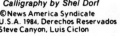

THINKS HE WILL BE A NATIONAL HERO, BUT HE MUST KNOW HE IS DEFENDING HIS COUNTRY JUST AS HORATIUS DID AT THE BRIDGE — OR WHEN SGT. YORK SOLOED IN WWI.

YOU WILL NEVER HAVE TO PLAY DAVID TO SOME CHARGING EXPLOSIVE GOLIATH BECAUSE THERE ARE MARINES AT ALL 150 U.S. EMBASSIES OUT THERE TO DO IT FOR YOU!

Calligraphy by Shel Dorf
©News America Syndicate
U.S.A. 1984, Derechos Reservados
Steve Canyon, Luis Ciclon

MILTON CANIFF

MY STUDIO IN NEW YORK OVERLOOKS THE N.Y.C. POLICE BOOTH OPPOSITE THE ENTRANCE TO THE UNITED NATIONS BUILDING. A WHISPER BY THE COP ON DUTY AT ALL TIMES INTO HIS (OR HER) PORTABLE-RADIO MIKE COULD SUMMON THE 22,855 ARMED MEMBERS OF THE CITY POLICE IN A MATTER OF MINUTES.

YESTERDAY THE OFFICERS ACKNOWLEDGED HOLIDAY GREETINGS IN A DOZEN LANGUAGES AS U.N. STAFF MEMBERS LEFT TO GO TO THEIR APARTMENTS FOR CHRISTMAS.

TODAY A 24-HOUR CORDON OF RIOT-TRAINED MANHATTAN POLICE SWAT TEAMS COULD BE SURROUNDING UNITED NATIONS PLAZA ...

BUT THE TERRORIST-CONTROL PEOPLE WILL PROBABLY BE AT HOME ENJOYING THE HOLIDAY WITH THEIR FAMILIES.

WHICH IS GREAT FOR THE UNITED NATIONS H.Q. IN NEW YORK.

IN SOME U.S. DIPLOMATIC COMPOUNDS AROUND THE WORLD IT WILL BE FULL-DANGER ALERT — AS USUAL.

CHRISTMAS DINNER DOES NOT GO DOWN SO EASILY WITH THE SOUND OF GUNFIRE IN THE CITY.

YOU OFFER PRAYERS FOR FRONT-LINE TROOPS — SPARE A FEW FOR THE SOLDIERS WHOSE ONLY WEAPON IS A WELL-WORN BRIEFCASE!

Calligraphy by Shel Dorf
©News America Syndicate, Steve Canyon, Luis Ciclon
U.S.A. 1985, Derechos Reservados

MILTON CANIFF

12/25

THERE WERE THESE CHARACTERS IN TRIPOLI WHO BIG-MOUTHED ABOUT HOW THEY RULED THE MEDITERRANEAN, AND ANY SHIPS IN THE AREA MUST PAY TRIBUTE TO THE LOCAL MOGULS.

THE BED-SHEET-ROBE CROWD GOT AWAY WITH IT FOR A TIME, BUT FINALLY, PRESIDENT THOMAS JEFFERSON SAID 'ENOUGH'.

HE SENT COMMODORE STEPHEN DECATUR TO AFRICA COMMANDING A NAVY TASK FORCE. IT DID THE JOB!

THAT'S HOW THE 'TRIPOLI' LINE GOT INTO THE MARINES' HYMN. THERE WAS NO 'OPEN' WAR GOING ON... JUST LIKE NOW.

BUT THE PROFESSIONALS WERE OUT THERE MINDING OUR BUSINESS — AS THEY ARE AT THIS VERY HOUR.

CHRISTMAS IS JUST ANOTHER DAY TO KEEP AN EYE ON THE BIG-MOUTHS — SO <u>WE</u> MAY BE MERRY — KNOWING THAT STEPHEN DECATUR'S VOICE IS STILL HEARD BY THE GOOD JOES STANDING WATCHES AROUND THE GLOBE!

MILTON CANIFF

Drop ↓

⑤
12/25
'87

THE STORY GOES THAT CHARLES KETTLING, THE ENGINEER-INVENTOR, ONCE TOOK A BRAND-NEW CAR OFF THE ~~PRODUCTION~~ PRODUCTION LINE, HAD IT HERMETICALLY SEALED IN A GLASS CASE AND PLACED IN THE LOBBY OF THE PLANT, WHERE IT COULD BE SEEN TWENTY-FOUR HOURS A DAY.

KETTLING WANTED THE EMPLOYEES WHO HAD WORKED ON THE BEAUTIFUL VEHICLE TO WATCH IT DETERIORATE WITHOUT BEING TOUCHED.

HE EXPLAINED THAT THE FINEST ~~PRODUCT~~ AUTOMOBILE MUST BE TESTED, CORRECTED AND RENEWED — AND THAT ONLY WAY TO LEARN HOW TO DO IT IS TO <u>USE</u> THE PRODUCT!

THERE WAS NO GLASS CASE IN 1776 AND 1777 SO THIS NATION HAS NOT BEEN FROZEN IN TIME. WE HAVE HAD OUR CIVIL WARS, WATERGATES, IRAN-SCAMS, DEFECTIONS TREASONS, FAILURE IN HIGH PLACES AND ALL THE OTHER FLESHLY FAILURINGS, BUT WE HAVE USED THE PRODUCT AND FOUND THAT IT HOLDS THE ROAD!

SHEL: YOU CAN BALANCE

AT CHRISTMAS — CONSTITUTION YEAR

SHEL: MORE SPACE

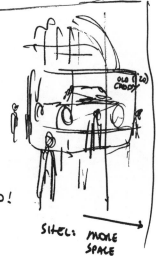
OLD ('26) CADDY

SHEL: BACK TO ME.

Milton Caniff's Rough Sketch for the 1987 Strip

Public Service Drawings

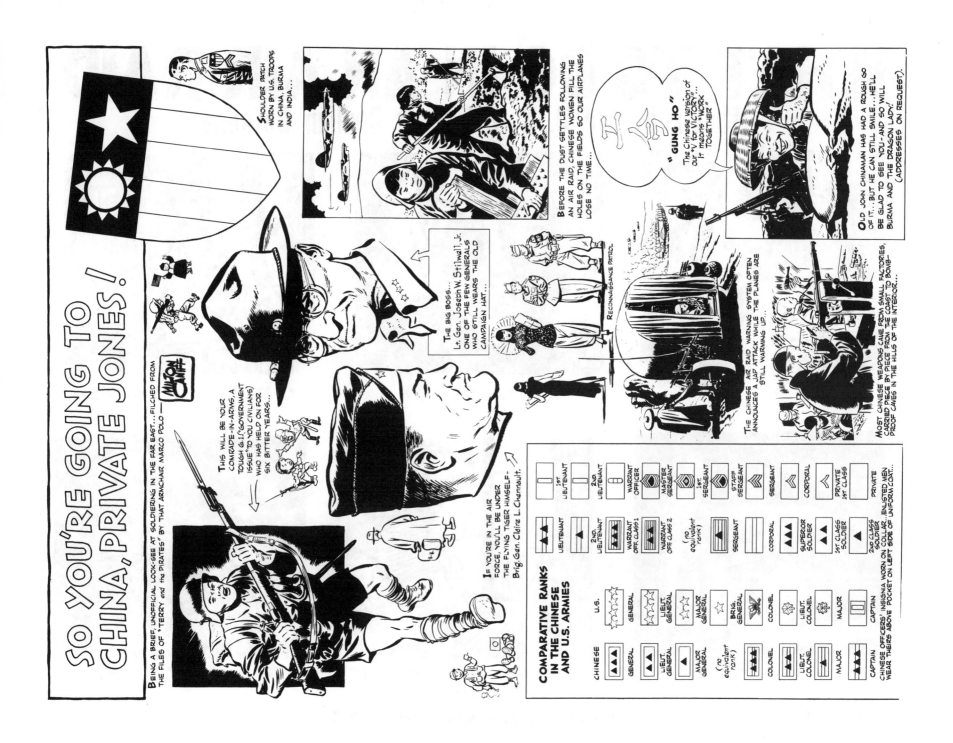

43

SO YOU'RE GOING TO CHINA, PRIVATE JONES!
BEING A BRIEF, UNOFFICIAL LOOK-SEE AT SOLDIERING IN THE FAR EAST... FILCHED FROM THE FILES OF "TERRY and the PIRATES" BY THAT ARMCHAIR MARCO POLO — MILTON CANIFF
SHOULDER PATCH WORN BY U.S. TROOPS IN CHINA, BURMA AND INDIA...
THIS WILL BE YOUR COMRADE-IN-ARMS, A TOUGH G.I. ("GOVERNMENT ISSUE" TO YOU CIVILIANS) WHO HAS HELD ON FOR SIX BITTER YEARS...
THE BIG BOSS... Lt. Gen. Joseph W. Stilwell, Jr. ONE OF THE FEW GENERALS WHO STILL WEARS THE OLD CAMPAIGN HAT...
IF YOU'RE IN THE AIR FORCE, YOU'LL BE UNDER THE FLYING TIGER HIMSELF- Brig. Gen. Claire L. Chennault.
BEFORE THE DUST SETTLES FOLLOWING AN AIR RAID, CHINESE WOMEN FILL THE HOLES ON THE FIELDS SO OUR AIRPLANES LOSE NO TIME...
RECONNAISSANCE PATROL
MP
工合
"GUNG HO"
The Chinese version of our "V for VICTORY"... It means "WORK TOGETHER"
COMPARATIVE RANKS IN THE CHINESE AND U.S. ARMIES
CHINESE
U.S.
GENERAL
GENERAL
LIEUT. GENERAL
LIEUT. GENERAL
MAJOR GENERAL
MAJOR GENERAL
(no equivalent rank)
BRIG. GENERAL
COLONEL
COLONEL
LIEUT. COLONEL
LIEUT. COLONEL
MAJOR
MAJOR
CAPTAIN
CAPTAIN
LIEUTENANT
1st. LIEUTENANT
2ND. LIEUTENANT
2ND. LIEUTENANT
WARRANT OFF. CLASS 1
WARRANT OFFICER
WARRANT OFF. CLASS 2
MASTER SERGEANT
(no equivalent rank)
1st. SERGEANT
SERGEANT
STAFF SERGEANT
CORPORAL
SERGEANT
SUPERIOR SOLDIER
CORPORAL
1st CLASS SOLDIER
PRIVATE 1st CLASS
2nd CLASS SOLDIER
PRIVATE
CHINESE OFFICERS' INSIGNIA WORN ON COLLAR... ENLISTED MEN WEAR THEIRS ABOVE POCKET ON LEFT SIDE OF UNIFORM COAT...
THE CHINESE AIR RAID WARNING SYSTEM OFTEN ANNOUNCES A JAP ATTACK WHILE THE PLANES ARE STILL WARMING UP...
MOST CHINESE WEAPONS CAME FROM SMALL FACTORIES, CARRIED PIECE BY PIECE FROM THE COAST TO BOMB-PROOF CAVES IN THE HILLS OF THE INTERIOR...
OLD JOHN CHINAMAN HAS HAD A ROUGH GO OF IT... BUT HE CAN STILL SMILE... HE'LL BE GLAD TO SEE YOU - AND SO WILL BURMA AND THE DRAGON LADY! (ADDRESSES ON REQUEST).

WHAT TO DO IN AN AIR RAID

Official—by the U. S. Office of Civilian Defense

1. KEEP COOL

2. STAY HOME

3. PUT OUT LIGHTS

4. LIE DOWN

5. STAY AWAY FROM WINDOWS

6. YOU CAN HELP

U. S. OFFICE OF CIVILIAN DEFENSE, Fiorello H. LaGuardia, Director. Washington, D. C.

HANDICAPPED WORKER

MILTON CANIFF

© 1968, Publishers-Hall Syndicate

CORDIAL FAMILY-STYLE CONGRATULATIONS TO **C.A.P.** ON ITS BIG **20**th ANNIVERSARY! *from* STEVE CANYON *and*

MILTON CANIFF

Copyright 1961, Field Enterprises, Inc.

WHY HIGH SCHOOL?

goodwill

"Good Willie"

STEVE CANYON   By Milton Caniff

PHYSICAL FITNESS IS IMPORTANT TO THE SECURITY OF OUR COUNTRY! THAT MEANS LOTS OF MILK AND DAIRY FOODS IN YOUR DIET!

— AND DON'T FORGET JUNE IS DAIRY MONTH .. ALL OVER AMERICA, Y'HEAR?

MILK

MILTON CANIFF

© 1962 by Field Enterprises, Inc.

MILTON CANIFF

JUNIOR CLASS ROCK BASH

MILTON CANIFF

—46—

Declaration of Dependence

"Were it left to me to decide whether we should have a government without newspapers or newspapers without government.... I should not hesitate a moment to choose the latter."

Th. Jefferson

FREEDOM OF THE PRESS
A Mandate From History

1976 NATIONAL NEWSPAPER WEEK
DEFEND THE 1st AMENDMENT

MILTON CANIFF

47

THEY SHALL NOT GROW OLD AS WE WHO ARE LEFT GROW OLD
AGE SHALL NOT WEARY THEM NOR THE YEARS CONDEMN.
AT THE GOING DOWN OF THE SUN — AND IN THE MORNING
WE SHALL REMEMBER THEM.
— Binyon

President's proclamation recalls D-Day valor

President Reagan issued a proclamation Thursday urging Americans to commemorate the valor of forces that landed on the Normandy coast 40 years ago in an assault that led to the liberation of Europe.

Reagan departed from Washington on Friday on a 10-day journey that will include a stop at Normandy on June 6, the 40th anniversary of the Allied invasion under the command of U.S. Gen. Dwight Eisenhower. In a written statement, Reagan recalled General Eisenhower's dramatic announcement from London: "People of Western Europe — a landing was made this morning on the coast of France by troops of the Allied Expeditionary Force . . . the hour of your liberation is approaching." Artist Milton Caniff made the above drawing especially for The Stars and Stripes.

As our book went to press Milton Caniff had just completed this drawing for the "No Greater Love" group in Washington, D.C. to call attention to the long neglected dead of the Korean War.

50

The Boy Scouts

Shown here at the age of 14, Eagle Scout Milton Caniff, started his career as a cartoonist at "Cricket Holler," the Scout camp of the Dayton, Ohio council. The camp newspaper, "Hodag," was the medium. It was a daily mimeographed newspaper.

THE MAKING OF AN EAGLE by MILTON CANIFF

FEW PEOPLE REALLY KNOW THE VALUE OF THIS
            SILVER BADGE.
IT MERELY TELLS THE WORLD YOU SET YOURSELF
            TO ONE AND TWENTY TASKS — AND PASSED THE TEST,
GIVING NO HINT OF WHY YOU CHOSE THIS COURSE
            INSTEAD OF LAZY SUMMERS ON THE BEACH,
THE REASON YOU DUG IN TO REACH THE VERY TOP
            RATHER THAN THROW THE PRECIOUS YEARS AWAY.
ELDERS FORGET HOW MUCH IT COSTS A BOY TO RISE
            ABOVE THE CROWD,
HOW EASILY A KID CAN JOIN THE GROUP AND HIDE.

A YOUNG MAN'S HOURS SPENT SCALING THE
            LONELY PEAK OF LEADERSHIP
TO REACH THE GOAL OF TEAM AND GROUP SUCCESS
            ARE COLORED BY THE MELANCHOLY FACT
THAT LOSING WILL BE BLAMED ON HIM ALONE.

NEVERTHELESS YOU SOUGHT THE HEIGHTS — AND NOW
            YOU HOLD THE SIGNED RECEIPT FOR HONORS WON
THE THRILL, THE GLOW OF FAMILY PRIDE IS HERE
            AND SHOULD BE SAVORED TO THE FULL.
BUT ALL THE EAGLE MEANS WILL NOT BE
            REALIZED TONIGHT,
IT MAY BE YEARS BEFORE YOU KNOW THE FINAL
            MEASURE OF ITS WORTH.

SOME DISTANT DAY WHEN SCHOLARS WRITE
            A JUDGMENT OF OUR TIMES,
THEY'LL SAY THAT FOR AWHILE YOUTH FALTERED
            AND WENT SOFT,
SCORNING THE VIRTUES WHICH, TILL THEN, HAD
            BUILT A NATION FROM THE RAWEST CLAY.
BUT WHEN THE WORLD'S DESPAIR HAD REACHED
            NEW DEPTHS,
A CALM AND SOLID CORE EMERGED — TO KEEP
            THE WAVERING ERA ON ITS COURSE.

THERE'LL BE NO MENTION IN THE BOOKS THAT
            YOU KEPT STRAIGHT
AND CHOSE TO LEAD — INSTEAD OF EASING OFF.

NOT ONE WILL TELL THAT YOU BECAME A MAN
            BEFORE YOUR TIME,
DURING THAT LAST, LONG STRETCH TO REACH THE
            EAGLE PEAK,
BUT YOU WILL KNOW WITHIN YOUR HEART THAT
            THIS WAS YOUR CONTRIBUTION TO THE CAUSE,
WHEN AN ENTIRE GENERATION STOOD ON TRIAL
            AND EARNED ITS PLACE IN HISTORY.

NEARLY EVERY MAN IN SERVICE IS ENTITLED TO CONGRATULATE YOU EAGLES WITH THE SCOUT SALUTE...

© Field Enterprises, Inc., 1969

BECAUSE MOST OF THEM ONCE WORE THE OTHER UNIFORM!

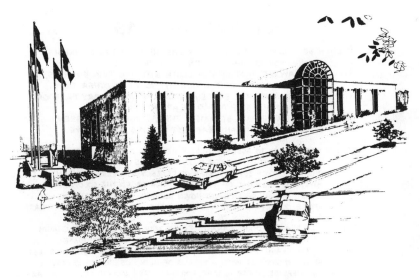

FLAG PLAZA

Flag Plaza and adjoining Scout Center represent impressive additions to downtown Pittsburgh's growing repertoire of fascinating attractions.

Located near the Civic Arena, this plaza and home of the nation's ninth largest Boy Scout Council, Allegheny Trails, is a showplace where the American flag and its ancestral predecessors are on continuous exhibit. Students of history will find no better source point for information regarding the origin and chronology of the flag than here. Boy Scout enthusiasts—and there are many of them—will, in the course of a visit, discover a bonanza of items relating to the worthy movement. And touring sightseers whose tastes guide them to inspiring and educational settings will certainly rate Flag Plaza and Scout Center as delighting.

Five flag poles, one of which towers to 80 feet, grace the plaza spanning out from the uniquely-designed Boy Scout building. On these sky-reaching supports fly, 24 hours around the clock, the American flag, flags of Pennsylvania and Pittsburgh, and the ensign of the Boy Scouts of America. One pole is reserved for historic American flags, and one of 30 of

these flags is changed at 7:30 p.m. each day during a colorful ceremony by a Pack, Troop or Post affiliated with the Boy Scouts. The historic flags depict past eras and episodes in American history.

An attractive garden shaped in a fleur-de-lis pattern in front of the flag stations provides a lasting tribute to all those former Boy Scouts who gave their lives in the service of their country.

These inspirational Flag Plaza adornments entice the visitor to explore the interior of the Scout Center building. No one doing this is disappointed. For the casual investigator, viewing the works of art on the first and second floors offers a rewarding experience. A life-size bronze casting of a typical Boy Scout, executed by Dr. Robert McKenzie, of Philadelphia, meets the visitor at the entrance way. The lobby features a "Tribute to Leadership" painting by Nat Youngblood, Art Director of the *Pittsburgh Press,* and a corner of the first floor is enhanced by the Lehman Memorial Reception Room. In the second floor Flag Room, artist Don Hewitt's carefully researched paintings of 30 historic American flags decorate the walls. Another attraction here is a life-size mural painted by Milton Caniff.

For those identified with the Boy Scouts—or for those who want to know more about them—all three floors of the building provide a treasure house of informative items and Scout-associated lore. The building is the activity center for 37,000 Boy Scouts and 13,600 adult volunteers, and it is the headquarters of the Allegheny Trails Council. Scout Executive George Cahill and his staff have offices in the building.

Flag Plaza and Scout Center stemmed from a search for a fitting memorial to the late Chester Hamilton Lehman. Mr. Lehman, a member of the founding family of Blaw-Knox, devoted considerable time to the Allegheny Trails Council and the Boy Scout movement. Both Flag Plaza and Scout Center are gifts from his wife, Vivian, in memory of his good work.

<u>YOU</u> ARE THE FLAG

AT EACH SUCCEEDING MILEPOST ON THE HISTORY TRAIL WHICH
    BRINGS YOU TO THIS MOMENT IN YOUR SPAN,
YOU'VE BEEN AWARE THAT BITS OF CLOTH, STITCHED INTO ENSIGNS,
    ARE THE SYMBOLS OF THE VIBRANT YOUTH OF OTHER DAYS,
WHO ANSWERED WHEN THE BURDEN FELL ON THEM TO CARRY FREEDOM'S
    TORCH ANOTHER STEP AHEAD OF APATHY AND FEAR;
WHEN AVARICE OR DESPAIR BECAME A THREAT TO WHAT HAD BEEN
    ACHIEVED BY TOIL AND EARNEST SEEKING TO IMPROVE.

IT NOW SEEMS EASY TO ASSUME THAT YOU'D HAVE RALLIED TO THE NEWBORN
    COLORS FLOWN AT BUNKER HILL AND IN THE COLD OF VALLEY FORGE,
BUT AGONIZING CHOICE DIVIDED MEN OF DECENCY AT EVERY MOMENT IN THE
    AWESOME SEQUENCE OF TRAVAIL WHICH FACED THE COLONIES,
AND SPAWNED A WAY OF LIFE UNKNOWN BEFORE YOUNG PATRICK HENRY
    SPOKE OUR INVOCATION IN A VOICE WHICH THUNDERS DOWN THE YEARS.

THE BATTLE FLAG OF DIXIE CANNOT TRULY TELL HOW DEEP THE CHASM
    IN THAT PHASE OF GLORY AND DEFEAT SO CLOSE TO HOME.
YET FROM THE CLASH OF BROTHERS CAME THE HOPEFUL BASTION OF A BREED
    ALONE IN CONFLICT WITH A WORLD OF BLIND OBEDIENCE TO POWER.
AS FREE MEN FALTER IN FAR PLACES, NOW THE STARS AND STRIPES LOOM LARGER
    AS THE DIKE OF HOPE AGAINST THE TIDES OF RED WHICH POUND OUR SHORES.

UNDER THIS MANTLE GREW THE REEDS AND MAYOS IN THE HEALING ARTS. WASHINGTON
    AND LINCOLN PIONEERED IN GOVERNMENT, NATIVE BORN AND GROWN.
BUSINESS PRODUCED A CARNEGIE AND FORD. ELLIOTT AND EINSTEIN FLOWERED IN
    THE FIELDS OF EDUCATION. CARVER AND SALK TOOK SCIENCE ROUTES TO
TRIUMPH AND RENOWN. THE WRIGHTS AND GLENN BROKE BOUNDS OF AIR, THEN SPACE
EDISON AND BELL GAVE VOICE AND EAR TO ALL MANKIND, WHILE WORSHIP,
FREE FROM FEAR, FOUND HAVEN HERE — ALLOWING MATHER AND CABRINI RIGHTS
    UNKNOWN IN OLD WORLD SHADOW PLACES.

IN THIS STILL VAST, REWARDING LAND, WHERE TROUBLE IS, AS ALWAYS,
    OPPORTUNITY DISGUISED IN WORKING CLOTHES...
WHERE, IN THE MIDST OF WAILS OF DISADVANTAGE AND DECAY,
    THERE YET ARISE UNSHACKLED MEN WHO SCOFF AT WHINING ODDS.
WE ARE A PEOPLE OF OUR OWN DESIGN AND PURPOSE — YOUNG ENOUGH A NATION
    THAT THE ATROPHY OF DISMAL PORTENT HAS NOT COOLED OUR ZEAL...
HENCE, IN THIS BLOODED HERALDRY THERE LIE UNFINISHED SEGMENTS
    OF A SCENE OF LONG HORIZONS, PAST AND FUTURE; THEN AND NOW

YOU'LL HEAR THE WEASEL WORDS OF HARPIES BENDING TO THE BLOW OF
    TEMPORARY HURT, BUT WHEN THE GOING'S TOUGH, THINK BACK
ON ALL THE YOUNG AMERICANS, MUCH LIKE YOU, WHO PASSED THE TEST
    WHEN BLEAKNESS DULLED THE FUTURE OF THEIR LAND.
THE TATTERED BANNERS SYMBOLIZE HOW WELL THEY STOOD AND HELD
    AGAINST THE FLOOD WHICH NEVER FULLY STOPPED, NOR EVER SHALL.

NOW THE DAY IS YOURS! DON'T WAIT FOR 'OTHER GUYS' TO DO THE JOB —
    TO CARRY HIGH THE HALLMARK OF OUR FAITH IN WHAT WE'VE WON.

THE 'OTHER GUY' IS <u>YOU</u>! — YOU <u>ARE</u> THE FLAG!!

AS IT APPEARS IN FLAG PLAZA,
PITTSBURGH — NARRATED BY JAMES STEWART

What <u>Is</u> Patriotism?

— A Sequence From Steve Canyon

STEVE CANYON

STEVE RETURNS TO THE UNITED STATES

HEY! MY FELLA IS ARDENT, BUT THOUGHTFUL...

...MEET ANOTHER WOMAN ON THAT EXOTIC MEDITERRANEAN ASSIGNMENT?

YES!

WHAT DO YOU MEAN?! —I'LL KILL THE WITCH!!

HOLD IT, GREEN EYES!

SHE'S THE CHILD WHO WAS KIDNAPPED...

...I AM WONDERING IF HER FATHER HAS GUARDS FOR HIMSELF...

...TO PREVENT HIM FROM MURDERING HER!

STEVE CHECKS IN AT HIS OFFICE

GENERAL CAMPHILL, I HAVE A REPORT ON---

IN DUE COURSE, MY BOY!...

...A LECTURE GROUP AT MAUMEE UNIVERSITY...

...HAS ASKED FOR A MILITARY PERSON..

..TO SPEAK CLOSE TO PEARL HARBOR DAY...

...ON PATRIOTISM!

HEY LOOK, SIR, I---

OF COURSE YOU WILL NOT BE ARMED!

REMEMBER WHAT HAPPENED AT KENT STATE!

© Field Enterprises, Inc., Chicago, Illinois, U.S.A. 1982, Derechos Reservados Steve Canyon Luis Ciclon   12-5

STEVE HAS BEEN ASSIGNED TO SPEAK TO A STUDENT GROUP ABOUT PATRIOTISM

Remember what happened to Nathan Hale!

LADIES AND GENTLEMEN... ...YOU ASKED FOR A PROFESSIONAL TO SPEAK TO YOU ON THIS VITAL SUBJECT!

THIS WILL NOT BE A CON JOB OR A SALES PITCH! IT IS A PERSONAL MATTER AND I'LL GIVE YOU MY PERSONAL OPINION!

SORRY THERE CAN BE NO QUESTIONS OR REBUTTAL BECAUSE I MUST CATCH THE LAST FLIGHT OUT OF THE LOCAL AIRPORT!

"PATRIOT... MEANS SOMEONE ZEALOUSLY DEVOTED TO HIS FATHER—OR TO HIS COUNTRY AS IN FATHERLAND.

..BUT IT DEPENDS ON WHICH COUNTRY! IN LA BELLE FRANCE AND MOTHER RUSSIA THE GENDER SHIFTS!

IRONY= IN ENGLAND IT ONCE MEANT A SEDITIOUS DISTURBER OF THE GOVERNMENT

FATHER WORSHIP—AS IN 'THE GODFATHER'—IS ALSO PATRIOTISM. IN OLD CHINA AND IN SICILY, THIS TOOK THE PLACE OF NATIONALISM.

IN EARLY TIMES SCOTCH AND IRISH CLANS DID THE SAME THING—YOU SUPPORT THE CHIEF AND HE'LL LOOK AFTER YOU!

THE AMERICAN COLONISTS CALLED THEMSELVES PATRIOTS, YET THEY WERE NEVER MORE BRITISH THAN WHEN THEY REBELLED AGAINST THE CROWN.

BUT TO QUOTE CHESTERTON= "SAYING 'MY COUNTRY, RIGHT OR WRONG!' IS LIKE DECLARING 'MY MOTHER, DRUNK OR SOBER'"

MOVING ALONG..

SO FAR—NO AIR FORCE RECRUITING PITCH! GUESS I'LL STICK AROUND!

CONTINUED...

12-12

12/13

"LADIES AND GENTLEMEN, I REPEAT— THIS WILL BE ONE PERSON'S VIEW ON PATRIOTISM!"

MAUMEE UNIVERSITY

"PATRIOTISM CAN BE STIRRED BY HATE AS WELL AS LOVE, ETHNICITY, GEOGRAPHY, RELIGION..."

"ADOLPH HITLER PLANNED TO USE THE 1936 BERLIN OLYMPIC GAMES AS A SHOWCASE FOR HIS CLAIM OF ARYAN (GERMAN) SUPERIORITY. JESSE OWENS, BLACK MAN FROM OHIO, RAN AWAY WITH THE SHOW! HITLER WALKED OUT..."

"YEARS LATER, WHEN OWENS RETURNED TO BERLIN, HE SAID,'THEY TELL ME MR. HITLER MEANT TO MAKE PROPAGANDA OF THE MEET—AND SNUBBED ME AFTER I WON FOUR MEDALS. I DON'T KNOW, I JUST CAME TO COMPETE—BUT I'M STILL HERE—AND MR. HITLER ISN'T!'"

STEVE IS SPEAKING ON PATRIOTISM

"PROPAGANDA USED TO AROUSE PATRIOTIC FERVOR IS OFTEN QUESTIONABLE...HITLER BURNED THE GERMAN REICHSTAG, WHICH ELIMINATED A GREAT SYMBOL OF THE OLD MODERATE REGIME..."

12/14

...TO A COLLEGE GROUP

"THE WORLD KNEW WHAT HAPPENED —BUT THE GERMAN PEOPLE (AT THE TIME) ACCEPTED THE STORY..."

ACH! THOSE ARSONIST JEWS!

HERR HITLER WILL SAVE US FROM THEM!

"THE SINKING OF THE BATTLESHIP 'MAINE,' IN 1898, PRODUCED A SLOGAN WHICH HELPED PRECIPITATE THE SPANISH-AMERICAN WAR—

REMEMBER THE MAINE!

"YET MANY THOUGHTFUL PEOPLE FEEL THAT THE EXPLOSION WAS JUST AS CAREFULLY CONTRIVED AS HITLER'S REICHSTAG FIRE!"

BUT, DEAR, THE SPANISH AREN'T MAD AT US!

THEY MUST BE! SEE—IT SAYS SO IN THE PAPER!

DEWEY DARE SPANISH

61

STEVE IS SPEAKING OF PATRIOTISM

"ENERGETIC YOUNG PEOPLE HAVE ALWAYS BEEN THE WELLSPRING OF SINCERE, UNQUESTIONING PATRIOTIC FERVOR...THE HITLER YOUTH ORGANIZATION WAS JUST THAT...

...TO A COLLEGE GROUP

12/15

"...SO WAS THE CHINESE RED GUARD.

凱旋

MILTON CANIFF

"AND OF COURSE, THE SOVIET RED YOUTH LEGIONS ARE ACTIVE IN THIS AREA."

EVEN THE U.S. BOY-AND GIRL-SCOUT MOVEMENTS SEEM TO ECHO SIMILAR ATTITUDES. BUT THERE IS ONE BIG DIFFERENCE... AMERICAN KIDS CAN QUIT ANY TIME THEY CHOOSE!!

"LOUDLY PUBLICIZED ACTS OF PATRIOTISM HAVE ALWAYS BEEN TARGETS FOR SKEPTICS, YET TWO IN THE SAME WAR HAVE REMAINED MILESTONES = THE CASE OF MAJOR JOHN ANDRÉ OF THE BRITISH ARMY...

MILTON CANIFF

12/16

STEVE IS SPEAKING TO A COLLEGE GROUP

"EVEN GEORGE WASHINGTON DID NOT WISH TO EXECUTE THE PERSONABLE ANDRÉ! THE COLONIALS TRIED TO ESTABLISH THAT HE WAS IN UNIFORM, HENCE ONLY A PRISONER OF WAR...

"BUT THE REDCOAT REFUSED TO LIE. HIS ONE REQUEST TO BE SHOT AS A SOLDIER, RATHER THAN HANG AS A SPY, WAS DENIED!"

AND NATHAN HALE, WHO WAS ARRESTED AS A SPY FOR GENERAL GEORGE WASHINGTON!

"MOST PEOPLE RECALL THE LAST WORDS OF NATHAN HALE— WHO NEVER DENIED BEING A SPY:

I REGRET THAT I HAVE BUT ONE LIFE TO LOSE FOR MY COUNTRY!

12/17

STEVE IS SPEAKING TO A COLLEGE GROUP

"BUT BEFORE HE WENT ON THE MISSION, CAPTAIN HALE TOLD A FRIEND:

I AM NOT INFLUENCED BY THE EXPECTATION OF PROMOTION OR PECUNIARY REWARD. I WISH TO BE USEFUL, AND EVERY KIND OF SERVICE NECESSARY TO THE PUBLIC GOOD BECOMES HONORABLE BY BEING NECESSARY. I AM FULLY SENSIBLE OF THE CONSEQUENCE OF DISCOVERY AND CAPTURE!

"PATRIOTISM, THEN, IS MORE OF THE HEART THAN THE HEAD.

GENERAL WASHINGTON, I WOULD STORM HELL IF YOU PLANNED IT!

ANTHONY, LET US BEGIN WITH STONY POINT!

"IT IS AN INVOLUNTARY MUSCLE OF THE SPIRIT, WHICH WE CAN'T CONTROL ANY MORE THAN WE CAN HELP FALLING IN LOVE WITH SOMEONE!"

"'PATRIOTISM' AND SELF-INTEREST ARE FREQUENTLY BLOOD BROTHERS UNDER THE METAPHOR! MEN FROM WISCONSIN AND MINNESOTA HAD LITTLE DIRECT INTEREST IN EMANCIPATING SLAVES...

12/18

STEVE IS SPEAKING TO A COLLEGE GROUP

BUT THEY FOUGHT LIKE TIGERS AT GETTYSBURG AND ELSEWHERE TO KEEP THE MISSISSIPPI OPEN AND FREE TO THE EAST COAST — SO THEY WOULD NOT HAVE TO PAY GOUGE PRICES TO THE NEW RAILROADS TO TRANSPORT THEIR GRAIN AND DAIRY GOODS.

"PATRIOTIC SENTIMENTS SELDOM JUST BURST FORTH. POLITICAL LEADERS LEARN EARLY WHERE TO LIGHT THE SPARK. WINSTON CHURCHILL DESCRIBED THE IMPENETRABLE BARRIER IMPOSED BY RUSSIA AS AN IRON CURTAIN TO AN AUDIENCE AT WESTMINSTER COLLEGE, MISSOURI!"

IF HE HAD INVENTED THE PHRASE IN WESTMINSTER, ENGLAND, IT MIGHT NOT HAVE EVEN MADE THE PRESS CABLES!

63

Panel 1:
12/20 STEVE IS SPEAKING ON THE SUBJECT OF PATRIOTISM...

STIRRING WORDS, RIGHTLY OR WRONGLY, INSPIRE PATRIOTIC ATTITUDE, BUT NOTHING DOES IT LIKE... MUSIC!

© Field Enterprises, Inc., Chicago, Illinois, U.S.A. 1982, Derechos Reservados Steve Canyon Luis Ciclon

...TO A COLLEGE GROUP

Panel 2:
"THE SUCCESSFUL CROWD MANIPULATOR, FROM A DANCE HALL OPERATOR WHO STOPS A RIOT BY PLAYING THE 'STAR SPANGLED BANNER'...

MILTON CANIFF

Panel 3:
"FROM 'RULE BRITANNIA' TO THE 'COLONEL BOGEY MARCH', THE BRITISH HAVE RALLIED TO THEIR VERY OWN MINSTRELSY!—AS IN 'THE BRIDGE OVER THE RIVER KWAI,' THE JAPANESE COMMANDER DID NOT RECOGNIZE THE DEFIANT TUNE WHISTLED BY HIS CHARGES, BUT HE KNEW HE WAS BEATEN ...

Panel 4:
" TO THE FRENCH COMMANDER WHO KNOWS JUST WHEN TO ORDER HIS MUSICIANS TO HIT THE 'MARSEILLAISE'!"

VERDUN

Panel 5:
"MUSIC, SPONTANEOUSLY OR DELIBERATELY, HAS MADE OR CHANGED THE COURSE OF HISTORY...FEW PEOPLE WOULD BE MOVED BY THE STRAINS OF THE OLDEST KNOWN SCHOOL SONG!..IT IS STILL IN USE AT WINSTON CHURCHILL'S ALMA MATER IN ENGLAND...

© Field Enterprises, Inc., Chicago, Illinois, U.S.A. 1982, Derechos Reservados Steve Canyon Luis Ciclon

12/21

Panel 6:
"BUT THE WHIFFENPOOF SONG GIVES YALE A CORNER-SALOON ALUMNI GROUP WHICH WOULD SURPRISE THE ARCHIVISTS AT NEW HAVEN ...

BA-A-A-A BA-A-A-A BA-A-A-AH

MILTON CANIFF

STEVE IS SPEAKING TO A COLLEGE GROUP

Panel 7:
AND MOST NORTH AMERICANS RESPOND TO THE FAMILIAR NOTRE DAME SONG WHETHER OR NOT THEY EVER SAW A FIGHTING-IRISH FOOTBALL TEAM

ECHOES HER NAME

Panel 8:
BUT THE GREATEST ROUSER IS TO HEAR THE REBEL YELL DECIBEL LEVEL RISE WHEN ANY AGGREGATION RIDES INTO

DIXIE!

"TO PUT IRONY ON THE ICING—'DIXIE,' THE GREAT RALLYING SONG OF THE CONFEDERACY (AND OF THE AMERICAN SOUTH EVER SINCE) WAS WRITTEN IN PITTSBURGH, PENNSYLVANIA, BY AN OHIO BOY NAMED DAN EMMETT!

12/22

MILTON CANIFF

STEVE IS SPEAKING TO A COLLEGE GROUP

"AND, BEING A STANDARD MINSTREL SHOW 'WALK AROUND'...

"IT WAS SUNG ALMOST AS EXTENSIVELY IN THE UNION ARMY CAMPS AS WITHIN THE CONFEDERATE LINES...

THE DIFFERENCE WAS...

"TO THE BLUECOATS IT WAS A PLEASANT, FOOT-TAPPING REMINDER OF NIGHTS IN THE HOMETOWN OPERA HOUSE IN HAPPIER TIMES."

"TO SOUTHERNERS, 'DIXIE' MEANT—

CHARGE!

12/23

"SO THE INCONGRUITIES OCCUR... 'AMERICA' EVOLVED FROM 'GOD SAVE THE KING'—THE 'STAR SPANGLED BANNER' MUSIC WAS A CASUAL ADAPTATION OF THE ENGLISH SONG 'TO ANACREON IN HEAVEN'.

IT'S A PATRIOTIC MARCH—TO THE TUNE OF 'ROCK OF AGES'!

"GEORGE SANTAYANA SAID: 'TO ME IT SEEMS A DREADFUL INDIGNITY TO HAVE A SOUL CONTROLLED BY GEOGRAPHY.'

REASONABLE THOUGHT FOR AN INTERNATIONALIST—MAN OF THE WORLD

STEVE IS SPEAKING TO A COLLEGE GROUP

"BUT PEOPLE WILL RETURN TO PLACES RAVAGED BY FIRE, FLOOD AND EARTHQUAKES—AND LIKELY TO BE AGAIN—BECAUSE 'THIS IS THEIR OWN, THEIR NATIVE LAND.'"

MILTON CANIFF

66

"OF COURSE, THE GOOD GUYS DO NOT ALWAYS WIN, HOWEVER DEEPLY DEVOTED TO A PATRIOTIC IDEAL. ...IT'S PARTLY HOW YOU LOOK AT IT—WHERE YOU SIT...MOST FRENCHMEN LOVED NAPOLEON.

STEVE IS SPEAKING TO A COLLEGE GROUP

"...YEARS LATER—HITLER WAS THE KNIGHT IN SHINING ARMOR TO THE GERMAN PEOPLE.

"PART OF THE INITIAL SUCCESS OF BOTH NAPOLEON AND HITLER WAS THE FACT THAT THEY HAD BEEN ARMY CORPORALS—AND KNEW THE PUBLIC MIND. THEY WERE MASTERS AT INSPIRING 'PATRIOTISM' IN THEIR FOLLOWERS.

MILTON CANIFF

"CLOSER TO HOME, THE MEMORY OF THE DEFEATED GENERAL ROBERT E. LEE IS REVERED IN BOTH NORTH AND SOUTH. ALL THREE MEN WERE CONSIDERED PATRIOTS. THESE THINGS ARE NEVER SIMPLE BLACK AND WHITE. THE SHADOW AREA DEPENDS ON WHERE YOU SIT WHEN THE SHOOTING STOPS!"

The BATTLE of GETTYSBURG
JULY 1·2·3 1863
DEDICATED TO ALL THE BRAVE MEN, NORTH AND SOUTH — WHO GAVE THEIR LIVES FOR THEIR COUNTRY

STEVE CANYON

by MILTON CANIFF

STEVE IS SPEAKING TO A COLLEGE GROUP ON PATRIOTISM

ABOUT PATRIOTIC HEROISM, G. C. LICHTENBERG SAID: "I WOULD GIVE SOMETHING TO KNOW FOR WHOSE SAKE PRECISELY...

"THOSE DEEDS WERE REALLY DONE THAT SUPPOSEDLY WERE DONE FOR THE FATHERLAND". —FAIR QUESTION! ONE ANSWER MIGHT BE WHAT NURSE EDITH CAVELL SAID IN BRUSSELS THE NIGHT BEFORE SHE WAS SHOT FOR HARBORING ESCAPING BRITISH SOLDIERS IN WORLD WAR ONE?

I REALIZE THAT PATRIOTISM IS NOT ENOUGH. I MUST HAVE NO HATRED OR BITTERNESS TOWARD ANYONE!

CALVIN COOLIDGE SAID: "PATRIOTISM IS EASY TO UNDERSTAND IN AMERICA. IT MEANS LOOKING OUT FOR YOURSELF BY LOOKING OUT FOR YOUR COUNTRY."

KEEP COOL W
COOLIDGE

ALSO SOMETIMES CALLED "ENLIGHTENED SELF-INTEREST"!

ONE OF THE BEST KNOWN COMMENTS ON THE SUBJECT IS: "PATRIOTISM IS THE LAST REFUGE OF THE SCOUNDREL!" —IT IS A STRONG INDICTMENT:

OH-H SAY CAN YOU SEE DAH DEE DUM DAH-DEE DAH-H

ONLY TROUBLE IS—AS DRYDEN POINTS OUT, SAMUEL JOHNSON WAS COMMENTING ON HOW SCOUNDRELS WILL USE THE CLOAK OF A USUALLY RESPECTABLE SENTIMENT TO COVER THEIR OWN DIRTY TRACKS! HE WAS NOT KNOCKING PATRIOTISM!

BRINGING IT INTO MODERN FOCUS...

...WHAT ABOUT WATERGATE? AMNESTY? VIETNAM?

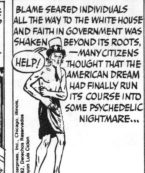

BACK IN THE 1920'S SOME PEOPLE WENT TO JAIL FOR TRYING TO RIP OFF AMERICAN TAXPAYERS BY STEALING NAVY OIL RESERVES FROM A PLACE CALLED TEAPOT DOME—

MR. SECRETARY, YOU ARE UNDER ARREST!

BLAME SEARED INDIVIDUALS ALL THE WAY TO THE WHITE HOUSE AND FAITH IN GOVERNMENT WAS SHAKEN BEYOND ITS ROOTS. —MANY CITIZENS THOUGHT THAT THE AMERICAN DREAM HAD FINALLY RUN ITS COURSE INTO SOME PSYCHEDELIC NIGHTMARE...

HELP!

THEN MOTHER WIT BEGAN TO REASSESS, LONG BEFORE PEARL HARBOR FUSED THE DOUBTERS INTO UNITED ATTITUDES; THE FAULT LAY WITH MERE MEN, WHO ABUSED THE RIGHT OF THEIR FELLOWS TO THE PURSUIT OF HAPPINESS.

IT'S ALL SO WON-DERFUL!

12-26

67

Alma Mater

TAKE YOUR CUE FROM THE CRUSADERS

A 1936 Cartoon by Milton Caniff

RUSH

THERE HAS BEEN NO MOMENT IN MY SPAN OF TIME,
COMPARED TO THAT BRIGHT SUNDAY WHEN
I TOOK THE SHIELD AND CROSS!
INITIATION AND THE BADGE WAS SOMETHING
ELSE—AND NOT TO BE COMPARED
TO WHAT IT MEANT TO PASS FROM BOY
TO MAN IN ONE BRIEF TICK OF TIME.

THE HIGH SCHOOL GLORY PASSED WAS PUT
WHERE IT BELONGED—FOR FOND RECALL.
NOW THE HUMBLING CHEMISTRY WHICH GUIDES
THE EGO URGE BEGAN ITS MAGIC EXERCISE.
NO LONGER HOME TOWN TRIUMPHS; LOCAL FAME!
THE COLLEGE CHALLENGE LOOMED IN AWESOME FACT.

A CLUTCH OF FRESHMEN JUST MY AGE, STRANGERS
UNTIL THAT MELDING LONG AGO.
'PLEDGE CLASS, SEPTEMBER: TWENTY-FIVE' IS LIKE
A BRAND ACROSS THE FADING RECORD BOOK.
NO MATTER IF WE STAYED THE ACADEMIC COURSE,
THAT CERTAIN DAY WE WERE A UNIT, PROUD AND FIRM,
SHARING THE FUN AND FAILURE, AND WE DO SO STILL,
AS IF THE CLOCKS OF MEMORY HAD STOPPED.

WHENEVER I OPEN THAT SPECIAL, PRIVATE TREASURE BOX
CONTAINING THE THINGS THAT MEAN THE MOST TO ME,
I HOLD THAT SIMPLE, TINY SHIELD AND CROSS
WHICH FELT A FULL TEN FEET TALL ON MY LAPEL
AND ONCE AGAIN IT'S AUTUMN AT OHIO STATE
—SOLEMN FACES ON THE ACTIVES—
ASKING ME IF I WOULD PLEDGE TO SIGMA CHI
—AND BE A KING FOR LIFE.

Special for the Sigma Chi (journalism fraternity).

...SPEAKING OF OHIO STATE

NOW IN MY DAY...

THERE IS SOME TIMELESS THREAD WHICH BINDS US TO THIS PLACE.
IT MUST BE MORE THAN COLORS, SONGS AND HALF-REMEMBERED NAMES!
WHEN FIRST I WALKED THE OVAL, FRIGHTENED, HOMESICK, UNPREPARED;
IT SEEMED IT ALL BEGAN THAT DAY... THAT NOT A SOUL HAD BEEN THIS WAY BEFORE.
MY ERA SCOFFED AT TALES OF GLORY PAST; OHIO FIELD AND OTHER ANCIENT LORE.

THEN, WHEN MY JUNE CAME—AND PUT THE MILES BETWEEN THE TOWN AND GOWN,
I THOUGHT THE BOOKS WERE CLOSED—IN FACT—AND IN THE AUDIT SENSE.
INSTEAD I FOUND MYSELF IN GROUPS WHOSE PRIMAL BOND WAS ALMA MATER SHARED;
WHERE AGE AND COLLEGE YEAR BECAME STATISTICS LAUGHED AWAY...
OUR COMMON NICHE 15th AND HIGH, WHEN FAILURE NEVER FAINTLY LOOMED.

NO CLASS BEFORE OR SINCE GIVES HOOT THAT MINE MARCHED OUT TO PANIC'S TUNE.
DEPRESSION CHANGED OUR LIVES, BUT TALK ABOUT IT BORES, SO LET IT PASS AWAY.
IMPORTANT IS THE FACT THAT ORTON'S CHIMES REACHED EVERY STUDENT EAR.
WHO CARES WHICH YEAR YOU MADE THE FIRST LONG TREK TO FINALS GRIND,
AGAINST THAT ARCTIC WIND WHICH ADDLED WITS ALREADY TURNED TO WHEY.

THE PLACES FAVORED ONCE FOR DATE AND DAWDLE GO EPHEMERAL WAYS...
BUT IN THEIR LITTLE SPAN THEY WERE COLUMBUS FOR THE LONG RECALL.
THOSE WARM RETREATS WHERE DREAMS BEGAN AND LOVE WAS CHRISTENED WITH A COKE.
IT LITTLE MATTERS WHETHER HERE OR GONE, NOSTALGIA MAKES THEM INNS OF ELEGANCE,
OUR MERMAID TAVERNS, FIT FOR STUDENT PRINCE, HOWEVER, PAUPERIZED.

YOU KNOW THE LINK IS THERE WHEN SOMEONE MAKES A MARK, ACHIEVES RENOWN;
AND THOUGH YOU'VE NEVER MET, YOU GLOW WITH PRIDE BECAUSE HE WENT TO STATE.
THAT DAY WILL COME FOR YOU ON CAMPUS NOW—IT'S BUILDING HOUR BY HOUR.
YOU'RE ANXIOUS TO GET ON WITH WHAT YOU'VE PLANNED—AND SCHOOL'S A DRAG....
BUT ON SOME FUTURE DATE THE FLASH WILL COME—THE GOOD OLD DAYS ARE <u>THESE!</u>
—SO USE THEM WELL!

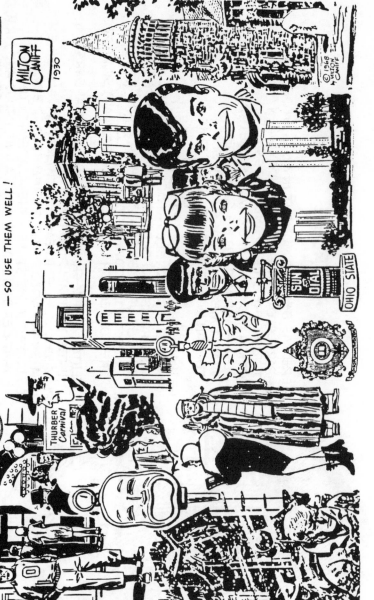

HOMECOMING

At each remembered name on this long listing
    of our dead,
I pause and try to reconstruct a mental picture of
    the being that I knew.
Reverie often fails and must be jogged by pictures
    in long untouched Makios.

Fresh faces, scrubbed to Spring Dance shine before
    the endless gray backdrop;
Clothing of another era, reflecting the eager fad
    that gave each fraternity porch
A look of carboned sameness as the girls strolled in
    review on fresh green Sunday afternoons.
How then can names upon a sombre listing tell of death
    when clocks of memory have already stopped?

The stern-faced captain of Marines who fell that
    bitter day on Tinian
Is not the dark young giant once I knew; it's just
    a slight coincidence in names.
My friend was gay, soft-hearted, hated to paddle
    freshmen not his size;
Thinking the scarlet sweater and the 'O' enough to
    speak his strength before all men.
He shall be always as I knew him then; bright flash
    of color across a rival goal;
Long legs stretched before the Chapter hearth;
    unwilling burner of the student lamp.

So, on those bright autumn Saturdays, when cars are
    mercifully stopped at campus gates,
I will take my place in that friendly web of people
    moving ever west across the Oval.
Unknown to me, for the most part, their colors join mine in
    the common plea for Ohio to do well today.
Among those thousands he must surely be, that one with
    whom I laughed goodbye so many Junes ago.
I'll not see him face to face; his seat is doubtless on
    the Olentangy side.
I will have to wait until the game is done.

Milton Caniff

73

INTEREST ACCOUNT

What does our University mean to you in
retrospect...forty; twenty; ten eons away?
Most of us would not have seen a college hall
without the heavy share Ohio paid, but now –
Even a sovereign state can't cover more than basic
costs for swelling freshman classes, year on year...
We lucky ones who passed our little time within
the sound of Orton's chimes are asked
To add the column of Remembrance...A total of
the dividends accrued on profits we've amassed
Because the accident of birth made entry to the
magic place a simple task.

No matter which accounting method points the
clear conclusion: it sums up that we owe a
Further tithe to ease the path for those who'll walk
the Oval on another day.

Few of us gave full measure of ourselves in student's
role; we seldom even knew quite how it's done.
In later time there is a chance to fill with coin of
realm the void we left by merely 'getting by.'

The principal amount can never be repaid because
it richens with the mellowing of memory,
we merely meet the interest on our debt, full
knowing who achieved the bargain on the deal!

74

Honoring The Air Force

THE BIRTH OF UNCLE BUD — LIEUT. P.G. COCHRAN, OBSTETRICIAN; (MIDWIFE)

for the great gang in the 65th FIGHTER SQUADRON... Their record since I met them at GROTON has been such as to make a land-bound scribbler feel honored to have had a small part in the building of the FIGHTING COCK TRADITION..... M.C.

NEW YORK, APRIL 3, 1944.

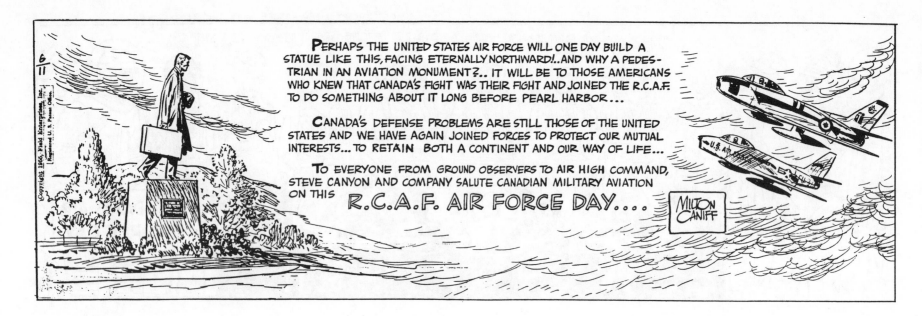

PERHAPS THE UNITED STATES AIR FORCE WILL ONE DAY BUILD A STATUE LIKE THIS, FACING ETERNALLY NORTHWARD!..AND WHY A PEDESTRIAN IN AN AVIATION MONUMENT?.. IT WILL BE TO THOSE AMERICANS WHO KNEW THAT CANADA'S FIGHT WAS THEIR FIGHT AND JOINED THE R.C.A.F. TO DO SOMETHING ABOUT IT LONG BEFORE PEARL HARBOR...

CANADA'S DEFENSE PROBLEMS ARE STILL THOSE OF THE UNITED STATES AND WE HAVE AGAIN JOINED FORCES TO PROTECT OUR MUTUAL INTERESTS... TO RETAIN BOTH A CONTINENT AND OUR WAY OF LIFE...

TO EVERYONE FROM GROUND OBSERVERS TO AIR HIGH COMMAND, STEVE CANYON AND COMPANY SALUTE CANADIAN MILITARY AVIATION ON THIS **R.C.A.F. AIR FORCE DAY....**

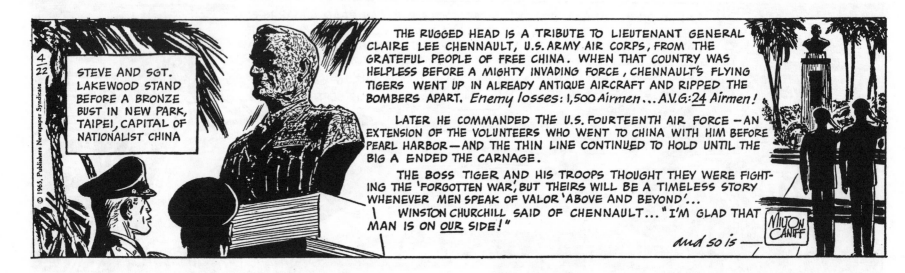

STEVE AND SGT. LAKEWOOD STAND BEFORE A BRONZE BUST IN NEW PARK, TAIPEI, CAPITAL OF NATIONALIST CHINA

THE RUGGED HEAD IS A TRIBUTE TO LIEUTENANT GENERAL CLAIRE LEE CHENNAULT, U.S. ARMY AIR CORPS, FROM THE GRATEFUL PEOPLE OF FREE CHINA. WHEN THAT COUNTRY WAS HELPLESS BEFORE A MIGHTY INVADING FORCE, CHENNAULT'S FLYING TIGERS WENT UP IN ALREADY ANTIQUE AIRCRAFT AND RIPPED THE BOMBERS APART. *Enemy losses: 1,500 Airmen...A.V.G.:24 Airmen!*

LATER HE COMMANDED THE U.S. FOURTEENTH AIR FORCE — AN EXTENSION OF THE VOLUNTEERS WHO WENT TO CHINA WITH HIM BEFORE PEARL HARBOR — AND THE THIN LINE CONTINUED TO HOLD UNTIL THE BIG A ENDED THE CARNAGE.

THE BOSS TIGER AND HIS TROOPS THOUGHT THEY WERE FIGHTING THE 'FORGOTTEN WAR', BUT THEIRS WILL BE A TIMELESS STORY WHENEVER MEN SPEAK OF VALOR 'ABOVE AND BEYOND'...
WINSTON CHURCHILL SAID OF CHENNAULT... "I'M GLAD THAT MAN IS ON OUR SIDE!"

and so is —

9/18

IN TWO MILITARY HEADQUARTERS A MESSAGE IS RECEIVED THAT STEVE CANYON IS ASHORE AT THE CASTLE OF LA HOOK — BUT IT READS SLIGHTLY DIFFERENTLY...

AT BRITISH H.Q.

FROM CANYON HIMSELF —HE SAYS HE WILL GO AFTER FLYING OFFICER HASTY — AND WE ARE NOT TO RISK AN INCIDENT WITH RED CHINA

AND AT RED CHINESE H.Q.

FROM AUSTRALIA... A RELIABLE SOURCE SAYS THAT BRITAIN, THE U.S. AND THE U.S.S.R. HAVE TROOPS ASHORE AT THE POINT WHERE MADAME HOOK RESIDES!

BUT APART FROM ALL THAT...

ONE OF THE REASONS WE ARE FIGHTING IN VIET NAM INSTEAD OF SAY, SEATTLE, IS THAT THE UNITED STATES AIR FORCE WAS BORN 18 YEARS AGO TODAY!

9/16

© 1967, Publisher's-Hall Syndicate

ON SEPTEMBER 18, 1947, THE VICTORIOUS, BUT WAR-WEARY, U.S. ARMY AIR CORPS WENT OUT OF EXISTENCE — WITH TWO GREAT WINS ON ITS VICTORY RECORD...

FROM IT AROSE AN ENTIRELY NEW FLYING SERVICE! ALREADY BLOODED IN TWO CONFLICTS, THE **UNITED STATES AIR FORCE** WILL BE TWENTY YEARS OLD NEXT MONDAY!

Dayton Air Force Hall Of Fame Portraits

CHARLES FRANKLIN KETTERING
1876 - 1958

BORN ON A FARM NEAR LOUDONVILLE, OHIO, KETTERIN
AN INNATE CURIOSITY ABOUT THE LAWS OF NATURE
THEIR APPLICATION TO SOLVING EVERYDAY PROBLE
A DEGREE IN ELECTRICAL ENGINEERING AT OHIO S
JOINED THE NATIONAL CASH REGISTER COMPAN
FECTED THE FIRST ELECTRIC CASH REGISTER AI
CHINES. LATER HE INVENTED AN IMPROVED IGNITI
FIRST ELECTRIC STARTER FOR AUTOMOBILES, WHI
FORMING DAYTON ENGINEERING LABORATORII
KNOWN AS "DELCO."

KETTERING'S INTEREST IN AVIATION BEGAN IN

HOWARD ROBARD HUGHES
1905 - 1976

SE INTEREST IN AVIATI
IIS TEENS. IN 1925 HE
IN 1930 PREMIERE
ED A WORLDWIDE

SPEED RECORD
PORTSMAN PILC
E BUILT HIS H-1 I
PANY AND IN W
N 1935 HE SE1
TES IN HIS NO
MON TROPHY.
IF 7 HOURS 28
ONTROL OF TRAI
938 HE AND A C
WORLD IN 3 [
ON AND COLLI
GAN THE DEVEL
ED THE DESIG

RICHARD EVELYN BYRD
1888 - 1957

OM AN EARLY AGE, BYRD W
Y. DURING WORLD WA
U.S. NAVAL AVIATI
ROVED NAVIGATI
FIRST TRA

ST
CA
GAGEL
LUDING
RETURN
AND SPI
SERVATIC

REUBEN HOLLIS FLEET
1887 - 1975

BECOMING INTERESTED IN MILITARY AVIATION WHILE SERVING IN THE
WASHINGTON STATE LEGISLATURE IN 1915, FLEET JOINED THE WASH-
INGTON NATIONAL GUARD AND WAS ASSIGNED AS A STUDENT TO ROCK-
WELL FIELD, CALIFORNIA, WHERE HE   WINGS IN AUGUST
1917.

AS CHIEF OF FLYING
VISED THE CONSTR
TION SECTION SCH
MAY 1918, THEN
BOARD AND WEN
ATTEND AN ADV
CONTRACT OI
SOLIDATED A
TRAINERS FC
FOR NATION
CONSOLID
MODORE'
PRODUCE
TRANSPO
MOVED T

HARRY FRANK GUGGENHEIM
1890 - 1971

AFTER TAKING PR
RECEIVED A CC
WITH THE U.S
WAR I.

IN 1925,
SCHOOL
ESTABLI
OF AEF
MODEL
VICE, A
STRATEI
SERVICE,
ORATOR
TED "BLI
AT SIX L
ADVISOR
OF THE D
SUPPORTE
GODDARD.
FLOYD BENN.
CARRIER STRIK
RANK OF CAPTAI
FLORENCE GUGGE!
TER AT THE CALIF

1917, GUGGENHEIM
VINGS AND SERVED
DURING WORLD

CLYDE VERNON CESSNA
1879 - 1954

N IOWA AND GROWING UP ON A KANSAS FARM, CESSNA EXHIBITED
IDE FOR MECHANICS AND BECAME AN EXPERT AT REPAIRING
NERY AND EARLY AUTOMOBILES. LATER, HE TOOK CHARGE
BILE SALES AND SERVICE AGENCY IN ENID, OKLAHOMA.
SIMPLICITY AND PERFORMANCE OF EARLY MONO-
LT HIS OWN AND TAUGHT HIMSELF TO FLY IT IN 1911.
THIS PLANE, HE USED IT IN EXHIBITION FLIGHTS
IND OKLAHOMA. MOVING TO WICHITA, KANSAS, HE
MONOPLANES AND USED
ES SIX- AND "COMET" MONOPLANES AND USED
CTURING COMPANY TO BUILD BIPLA
IS UNTIL WORLD WAR I, IN 1925, HE H
1926, HE DEVELOPED AN ADVAN
CITY OF OAK! AND" AND TH
S IN

81

FRANK BORMAN
1928 -

LEARNING TO FLY AT THE AGE OF 15, BORMAN LATER ATTENDED THE U.S. MILITARY ACADEMY AND EARNED HIS AIR FORCE WINGS IN 1951. AFTER SERVING WITH THE 44TH FIGHTER-BOMBER SQUADRON AND INSTRUCTING AT AIR FORCE WEAPON SCHOOLS, HE RECEIVED A MASTER'S DEGREE IN AERONAUTICAL ENGINEERING FROM THE CALIFORNIA INSTITUTE OF TECHNOLOGY AND BECAME AN ASSISTA... ...AT THE U.S. MILITARY ACADEMY. UPON COMP... ...PILOT SCHOOL AT EDWARDS A.F.B., HE S... ...ROJECT OFFICER AND TEST PILOT

SELECTED ... ...TRATION IN 1962 FOR ... ...MINI-7 MIS-SION T... ...EARTH ORBIT... ...VED ON THE A... ...SPAC... ...OGRAM CREW... ...POLLO THEN ... ...HIS TO T... ...HEY ...ART... ...HE A...

EDWARD VERNON RICKENBACKER
1890 - 1975

...NTERESTED IN AUTOMOBILES FROM AN EARLY AGE, RICK... BECAME A MECHANIC AND, IMBUED WITH RACING, BECAME... RACE CAR DRIVER. WHEN THE UNITED STATES ENTERED TH... HE TRIED TO ORGANIZE AN AERO SQUADRON OF HIS... FRIENDS.

RICKENBACKER ENLISTED IN THE AVIATION SECTION... CORPS AND REPORTED FOR FLIGHT INSTRUCTIONS... COMPLETING AERIAL GUNNERY SCHOOL, HE WAS... FRENCH AIR SQUADRON. IN 1918 HE REPORTED TO... RING" 94TH AERO SQUADRON. HE SHOT DOWN HIS F... PLANE ON APRIL 29 AND BECAME AN "ACE" ON MAY 3... SEVEN ENEMY AIRPLANES ON SEPTEMBER 25, LATER... CONGRESSIONAL MEDAL OF HONOR. HE BECAME CO... FICER OF THE 94TH, AND BY THE END OF THE WAR HE... LEADING "ACE" WITH 22 AIRPLANES AND 4 BALLOONS... AFTER THE WAR HE RETURNED TO THE AUTOMOTIVE BI... HE BECAME ASSOCIATED WITH SEVERAL AIRCRAFT COM... THEIR EARLY YEARS OF DEVELOPMENT AND ASSISTED... TION AND GROWTH OF SEVERAL MAJOR AIRLINES. DURING... II. WHILE ON A SPECIAL MISSION, HIS AIRPLANE WAS FORCE...

AMELIA EARHART PUTNAM
1897 - 1937?

LEARNING TO FLY IN 1921, AMELIA EARHART ACCUMULATED AN IMPRESSIVE NUMBER OF HOURS IN THE AIR BEFORE BECOMING FAMOUS AS THE FIRST WOMAN TO FLY ACROSS THE ATLANTIC AS A PASSENGER IN 1928. EMBARKING UPON AN EXTENSIVE FLYING CAREER, SHE MADE THE FIRST RECORDED WOMAN'S SOLO FLIGHT ACROSS THE CONTINENT IN 1929 AND PARTICIPATED IN THE FIRST "POWDER PUFF DERBY" OF THE NATIONAL AIR RACES. AFTER SETTING NUMEROUS SPEED RECORDS, SHE BEGAN A CAREER IN COMMERCIAL AVIATION AND HELPED PROMOTE WOMEN'S INTEREST IN AIR TRAVEL. IN 1933 SHE BECAME THE FIRST WOMAN TO PILOT AN AUTOGIRO, SETTING AN ALTITUDE RECORD AND ALSO MAKING A SOLO EXHIBITION TOUR ACROSS THE COUNTRY.

IN 1932 AMELIA EARHART BECAME THE F... SOLO FLIGHT ACROSS THE ATLAN... TO IRELAND. A PARTICIPANT IN... 1930'S, SHE WAS THE FIRST V... TINENTAL FLIGHT IN 1932... TINENTAL SPEED REC... FLIGHT FROM HAWAII... WILL FLIGHT FROM L... NEWARK, NEW JERS... WORLD WITH A NAVI... THE ATLANTIC, AFRIC... ON A FLIGHT TO HO...

AMELIA EARHART PUT... FOR OUTSTANDING C... PROMOTION OF THE I... NUMEROUS RECORDS... TINENTAL AND TRANSO...

WILLIAM EDWARD BOEING
1881 - 1956

ALREADY A SUCCESSFUL LUMBERMAN WHEN HE BECAME INTERESTED IN AERONAUTICS IN 1910, BOEING TOOK FLYING LESSONS IN 1915. HE THEN HELPED DESIGN AND BUILD TWO "B&W" SEAPLANES, ONE OF WHICH HE SUCCESSFULLY FLEW IN 1916.

AFTER DECIDING TO MANUFACTURE AIRPLANES, BOEING ESTABLISHED THE PACIFIC AERO PRODUCTS COMPANY IN 1916, WHICH BECAME THE BOEING AIRPLANE COMPANY A YEAR LATER. DURING WORLD WAR I HIS COMPANY BUILT TRAINER-TYPE SEAPLANES FOR THE NAVY. AFTER THE WAR, THE STRUGGLING COMPANY ENGAGED IN DIVERSE ACTIVITIES. IN 1919 HE MADE ONE OF THE FIRST INTERNATIONAL AIRMAIL FLIGHTS BETWEEN CANADA AND THE UNITED STATES. HIS COMPANY PRODUCED THE FIRST OF A SUCCESSFUL LINE OF ARMY PURSUIT AND NAVY CARRIER FIGHTER PLANES IN 1923. UPON BEING AWARDED THE CHICAGO-SAN FRANCISCO AIR MAIL CONTRACT IN 1926, HE ESTABLISHED THE BOEING AIR TRANSPORT SERVICE AND BUILT A FLEET OF PLANES WITH WHICH HE INAUGURATED MAIL AND PASSENGER SERVICE IN 1927. HE SERVED AS CHAIRMAN OF THE UNITED AIRCRAFT AND TRANSPORT COMPANY AND IN 1934 WAS AWARDED THE DANIEL GUGGENHEIM MEDAL. HIS COMPANY SUBSEQUENTLY BECAME A PIONEERING LEADER IN THE MANUFACTURE OF MULTI-ENGINE AIRCRAFT, COMMERCIAL JET TRANSPORTS, AND SPACE VEHICLES.

WILLIAM EDWARD BOEING WAS ENSHRINED ON DECEMBER 15, 1966, FOR OUTSTANDING CONTRIBUTIONS TO AVIATION BY HIS SUCCESSFUL ORGANIZATION OF A NETWORK OF AIRLINE ROUTES AND THE PRODUCTION OF VITALLY IMPORTANT MILITARY AND COMMERCIAL AIRCRAFT.

T. CLAUDE RYAN
1898 - 1982

...V FROM BOYHOOD, RYAN TOOK FLYING... WAR I AND IN 1920 ENLISTED IN THE ARMY... ORMED THE RYAN FLYING COMPANY TO... IG SERVICES, AND IN 1925 ESTABLISHED... O AIR LINE, THE FIRST YEAR-ROUND...

...AIRLINES, INC., AND BEGAN THE... AIRMAIL PLANES. HIS M-1 MONO-... SERVED ON MANY EARLY AIRMAIL... OLVED THE FAMOUS "SPIRIT OF ST.... THE "S-T" SPORTS-TRAINER, AND... IG PRIMARY TRAINERS, INCLUDING... E NAVY NR-1. DURING WORLD WAR... UTICS TRAINED 14,000 ARMY AIR... RONAUTICAL COMPANY DESIGNED... THE NAVY'S FIRST JET FIGHTER.... TURED THE "NAVION" LIGHTPLANE... "FIREBIRD" WAS THE FIRST AIR-TO-... 952 HIS "FIREBEE" FLYING TARG... 957 HIS X-13 "VERTIJET"... EOFF AND LANDING F... TIFAN" AIRCRAFT... EROSPACE ELEC... OPED THE RA... O 11 LUNAR...

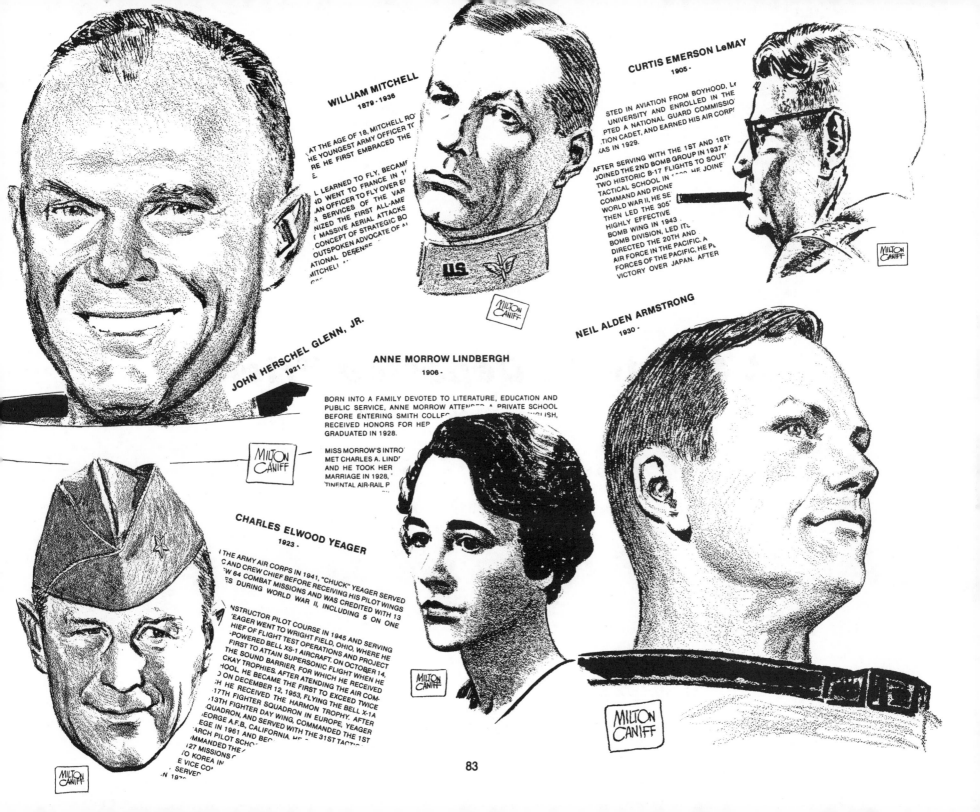

WILLIAM MITCHELL
1879 - 1936

AT THE AGE OF 18, MITCHELL RO
HE YOUNGEST ARMY OFFICER TO
RE HE FIRST EMBRACED THE

L LEARNED TO FLY, BECAM
D WENT TO FRANCE IN 1
AN OFFICER TO FLY OVER E
R SERVICES OF THE VAR
NIZED THE FIRST ALL-AME
MASSIVE AERIAL ATTACK
CONCEPT OF STRATEGIC BO
OUTSPOKEN ADVOCATE OF
ATIONAL DEFENSE
MITCHELL

CURTIS EMERSON LeMAY
1905 -

STED IN AVIATION FROM BOYHOOD, L
UNIVERSITY AND ENROLLED IN THE
PTED A NATIONAL GUARD COMMISSIO
TION CADET, AND EARNED HIS AIR CORP
AS IN 1929.

AFTER SERVING WITH THE 1ST AND 18TH
JOINED THE 2ND BOMB GROUP IN 1937 A
TWO HISTORIC B-17 FLIGHTS TO SOUT
TACTICAL SCHOOL IN   HE JOINE
COMMAND AND PIONE
WORLD WAR II, HE SE
THEN LED THE 305
HIGHLY EFFECTIVE
BOMB WING IN 1943
BOMB DIVISION, LED IT
DIRECTED THE 20TH AND
AIR FORCE IN THE PACIFIC, A
FORCES OF THE PACIFIC, HE P
VICTORY OVER JAPAN. AFTER

JOHN HERSCHEL GLENN, JR.
1921 -

ANNE MORROW LINDBERGH
1906 -

BORN INTO A FAMILY DEVOTED TO LITERATURE, EDUCATION AND
PUBLIC SERVICE, ANNE MORROW ATTENDED A PRIVATE SCHOOL
BEFORE ENTERING SMITH COLLE   NGLISH,
RECEIVED HONORS FOR HER
GRADUATED IN 1928.

MISS MORROW'S INTRO
MET CHARLES A. LIND
AND HE TOOK HER
MARRIAGE IN 1928,
TINENTAL AIR-RAIL P

NEIL ALDEN ARMSTRONG
1930 -

CHARLES ELWOOD YEAGER
1923 -

THE ARMY AIR CORPS IN 1941, "CHUCK" YEAGER SERVED
C AND CREW CHIEF BEFORE RECEIVING HIS PILOT WINGS
W 64 COMBAT MISSIONS AND WAS CREDITED WITH 13
S DURING WORLD WAR II, INCLUDING 5 ON ONE

NSTRUCTOR PILOT COURSE IN 1945 AND SERVING
YEAGER WENT TO WRIGHT FIELD, OHIO, WHERE HE
HIEF OF FLIGHT TEST OPERATIONS AND PROJECT
POWERED BELL XS-1 AIRCRAFT. ON OCTOBER 14,
FIRST TO ATTAIN SUPERSONIC FLIGHT WHEN HE
THE SOUND BARRIER, FOR WHICH HE RECEIVED
CKAY TROPHIES. AFTER ATENDING THE AIR COM
HOOL. HE BECAME THE FIRST TO EXCEED TWICE
ON DECEMBER 12, 1953, FLYING THE BELL X-1A
H HE RECEIVED THE HARMON TROPHY. AFTER
17TH FIGHTER SQUADRON IN EUROPE, YEAGER
13TH FIGHTER DAY WING, COMMANDED THE 1ST
QUADRON, AND SERVED WITH THE 31ST
EORGE A.F.B., CALIFORNIA
EGE IN 1961 AND BEC
ARCH PILOT SCHO
MMANDED THE
27 MISSIONS
TO KOREA IN
E VICE CO
SERVED
N 197

83

A Salute To Departed Friends

Panel 1:
WHAT'S ALL THIS? WE'RE SUPPOSED TO BE IN CHINA!

...BUT IT LOOKS LIKE CHICAGO!

IS MIRACLE! IS SPOOKY! IS SHOO MIKE FANTASTICAL!

Panel 2:
WHAT'S THE IDEA, CANIFF? YOU CAN'T BREAK UP CONTINUITY THIS WAY!

OH YES I CAN, BOYS! THIS IS REALLY SPECIAL...

Panel 3:
...IT'S JOHN McCUTCHEON'S 50TH ANNIVERSARY AS A SIGMA CHI — AND WE'RE GOING TO BE THERE TO WISH HIM WELL! — REMEMBER, IF IT HADN'T BEEN FOR HIM THERE WOULD BE NO "TERRY AND THE PIRATES" — SO TURN ON THE GRATITUDE!

OKAY! HERE GOES...

Panel 4:
... SALUTE THE ESCUTCHEON OF BROTHER McCUTCHEON — COME, FILL UP YOUR BUMPERS AND DRINK! IF IT WEREN'T FOR JOHN T. THERE'S NO DOUBT THAT WE'D BE JUST SOME DROPS IN A BOTTLE OF INK!

IT IS NO SECRET THAT MANY CHARACTERS IN THIS STRIP HAVE BEEN PATTERNED AFTER REAL PEOPLE.. GENERAL SHANTY TOWN AND, DURING THE WAR, COL. VINCE CASEY, WERE FICTIONAL COUNTERPARTS OF CLINTON D. VINCENT, WEST POINT '36, WHO WAS A GENERAL AT THE AGE OF 29.

TODAY IN YUMA, ARIZONA, THE U.S.A.F. ROCKET RANGE WILL BE RENAMED VINCENT AIR FORCE BASE AFTER THIS REMARKABLE MAN WHO DIED OF OVERWORK WHILE STRUGGLING TO HELP PERFECT A SYSTEM THAT WILL KEEP A POTENTIAL ENEMY FROM EVER VIOLATING THE NORTH AMERICAN CONTINENT.

WHY DID HE DO IT? FOR THE SAME REASON ANY MAN WOULD THROW HIMSELF BETWEEN HIS FAMILY AND AN ARMED INTRUDER IN HIS HOUSE.

CASEY VINCENT WAS ONLY 40 YEARS OLD WHEN HE DIED ON THE EVE OF A BIG, NEW JOB......ALL HONOR TO HIS NAME!

EXCUSE ME...THIS IS PERSONAL...

5/28

As MANY OF YOU ALREADY KNOW, THE WORDS IN CARTOON STRIPS ARE SCRIBBLED IN PENCIL BY THE WRITER, THEN CAREFULLY GONE OVER IN INK BY SPECIALISTS IN THE CRAFT.

SUCH WARM AND READABLE TEXTS SET THE TONE FOR THE DRAWING — AND MAKE IT EASY FOR YOU TO READ AND ENJOY THE TOTAL FEATURE.

NEARLY EVERY WORD IN TERRY, MALE CALL AND STEVE CANYON WAS LOVINGLY LETTERED BY FRANK ENGLI
— WHO WAS ALSO A SKILLED COMIC ARTIST ON HIS OWN.
FRANK DIED RECENTLY, AFTER A LONG, PUNISHING ILLNESS. HIS WORK WAS UNIQUE; HE WAS WIDELY COPIED.
BUT THE GREATEST ACCOLADE A NEWSPAPER CARTOONIST CAN EARN IS =

HE NEVER MISSED A DEADLINE!

SO LONG, EAGLE-EYE

MILTON CANIFF

12/19

MAYBE THIS IS THE PLACE FOR A PERSONAL NOTE...

IT WAS FUN PRETENDING THAT STEVE CANYON WAS WITH THE WRIGHT BROTHERS AT KITTY HAWK...
BUT ON THE SERIOUS SIDE, THEIR FLIGHT CHANGED THE WORLD AND TOUCHED THE LIVES OF EVERYONE IN IT.
IT IS HARD TO BELIEVE THAT A MERE 15 YEARS AFTER DECEMBER 17, 1903, I SAT NEAR McCOOK FIELD IN DAYTON, OHIO AND WATCHED VETERANS OF THE 1914 – 1918 AIR SERVICE BEGIN TO MOLD THE MIGHTY U.S. AIR FORCE OF TODAY.
EVEN STRANGER TO RECALL... I ACTUALLY KNEW ORVILLE WRIGHT!

MILTON CANIFF

THE NAZIS COULDN'T DO IT... THE JAPANESE FAILED...THEN, ON AUGUST 25 IT HAPPENED! PHIL COCHRAN IS DEAD! —WITH HIS BOOTS ON...RIDING WITH HIS HUNT CLUB! HE HAD NEARLY EVERY MEDAL IN THE BOOK—EXCEPT THE PURPLE HEART!

SO FLIP CORKIN AND GENERAL PHILERIE GO WITH HIM. I ONCE ASKED PHIL HOW HE HANDLED IT WHEN A GOOD FRIEND FAILED TO RETURN FROM A COMBAT MISSION. "WE ALWAYS CONTINUED TALKING ABOUT HIM AS IF HE HAD GONE ON TO ANOTHER ASSIGNMENT!" HANG IN, 'FEELEEP!' I'LL SEE YOU AROUND— *Milton*

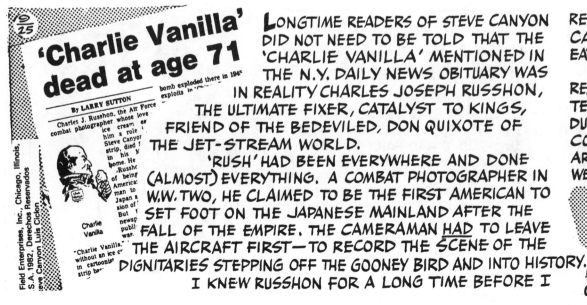

'Charlie Vanilla' dead at age 71

By LARRY SUTTON

Charles J. Russhon, the Air Force combat photographer whose love ice cream... him a role... Steve Canyon strip, died... home. He... Russho... of being... Americas... man to... Japan a... sion of... But... newsp... publi... war...

Charlie Vanilla

"Charlie Vanilla," without an ice c... in cartoonis... strip ba...

bomb exploded there in 194... exploits in...

LONGTIME READERS OF STEVE CANYON DID NOT NEED TO BE TOLD THAT THE 'CHARLIE VANILLA' MENTIONED IN THE N.Y. DAILY NEWS OBITUARY WAS IN REALITY CHARLES JOSEPH RUSSHON, THE ULTIMATE FIXER, CATALYST TO KINGS, FRIEND OF THE BEDEVILED, DON QUIXOTE OF THE JET-STREAM WORLD.

'RUSH' HAD BEEN EVERYWHERE AND DONE (ALMOST) EVERYTHING. A COMBAT PHOTOGRAPHER IN W.W. TWO, HE CLAIMED TO BE THE FIRST AMERICAN TO SET FOOT ON THE JAPANESE MAINLAND AFTER THE FALL OF THE EMPIRE. THE CAMERAMAN HAD TO LEAVE THE AIRCRAFT FIRST—TO RECORD THE SCENE OF THE DIGNITARIES STEPPING OFF THE GOONEY BIRD AND INTO HISTORY. I KNEW RUSSHON FOR A LONG TIME BEFORE I

REALIZED THAT I WAS SITTING ON A GREAT CARTOON PERSONALITY! I DREW HIM ALWAYS EATING AN ICE-CREAM CONE, HIS FAVORITE FOOD.

IT IS A GREAT WRENCH TO ME WHEN VIVID REAL-LIFE COUNTERPARTS OF MY CARTOON CHARACTERS LEAVE THE STAGE. I'LL BET THAT RIGHT NOW DUDE HENNICK, VINCE CASEY, MAC DAVEY, FLIP CORKIN, GENERAL PHILERIE AND CHARLIE VANILLA ARE SOMEWHERE 'HANGAR FLYING' ABOUT WHEN THEY WERE ALL IN THE FUNNY PAPERS! *Milton Caniff*

YOU KNEW OF **FRED WARING** AS THE FAMOUS ORCHESTRA AND CHORAL LEADER WHO THRILLED PEOPLE FOR YEARS AS HE AND HIS PENNSYLVANIANS INTERPRETED THE WORLD'S MUSIC.

PRESENT AND FORMER MEMBERS OF THAT GROUP CAME FROM EVERY-WHERE TO SING AT HIS FUNERAL.

YOU WERE PROBABLY NOT AWARE THAT FRED WAS ONE OF THE FOREMOST NEWSPAPER CARTOON BUFFS AND COLLECTORS. ON TOUR, LATE EDITIONS FROM EVERY CITY WERE DELIVERED TO

HIM ON THE BUS—SO HE COULD FOLLOW THE COMICS... ALL THE COMICS!

NOW OUR #ONE FAN IS GONE. CARTOONISTS WORKING THE LONG NIGHT HOURS WILL HEAR THOSE OLD, GREAT RECORDINGS ON RADIO AND HOPE THAT FRED WARING IS HAVING PEACEFUL *SLEEP, SLEEP, SLEEP*

10-15

MOST OF US HAVE A PERSON OUTSIDE OUR FAMILIES WHO HAS A PROFOUND IN-FLUENCE ON OUR LIVES... MINE WAS **MARTHA K. SCHAUER** THIS STATELY LADY TAUGHT HIGH SCHOOL ART TO THE USUAL KNUCKLE-HEAD CROWD! SHE GRADED EACH STUDENT AGAINST HIMSELF (NOT THE CLASS AVER-AGE). IF SHE THOUGHT I WAS GOOFING OFF, SHE CUT MY USUAL **A** DOWN TO **B** —AND I GOT THE MESSAGE! M.K.S. DECLARED THAT EVERYTHING WE COULD SEE EXCEPT THE NATURAL

ELEMENTS WAS DESIGNED BY SOMEONE! SHE DEFINED ART AS SOMETHING WHICH WOULD INSPIRE PEOPLE TO PAY A LOT OF MONEY TO OWN.

JUST BEFORE GRADUATION SHE CALLED ME INTO HER OFFICE AND SAID I HAD FAILED IN MY POTENTIAL—AND THAT ANY PERSON WITH TALENT WHO DID NOT DEVELOP IT TO THE FULLEST DESERVED TO BE PUNISHED. "I WOULD LICK YOU IF I COULD!"

MARTHA SCHAUER DIED AT AGE 96. NOW I AM ON MY OWN.

Armed Forces Day Strips

5-19

WHY DID YOU SLEEP SO WELL LAST NIGHT, CITIZEN?
— BECAUSE YOU KNEW THERE WERE AIR FORCE MEN AWAKE, ALERT FOR THE WORD TO GO ANYWHERE IN THE WORLD TO PROTECT YOU FROM ATTACK ...

WHY DID YOU SEND YOUR KIDS OFF TO SCHOOL WITH SUCH CONFIDENCE TODAY? BECAUSE THERE ARE NAVY MEN ON PATROL ON EVERY OCEAN, READY TO REPEL AN ATTACK BY SEA OR AIR...

WHY DIDN'T YOU GET PANICKY AT THE NEWS FROM ABROAD? BECAUSE THERE ARE MARINES READY TO LAND AT ANY SPOT AND STOP TROUBLE BEFORE IT STARTS, AS THEY HAVE DONE IN ASIA...

AND WHY ARE YOU JUST PLAIN PROUD? BECAUSE THE ARMY IN KOREA HAS PROVED THAT AMERICANS WILL DIE TO HALT ANY THREAT TO FREEDOM IN 1951 — AS THEY HAVE DONE SINCE 1776!

ARMED FORCES DAY · MAY 19, 1951

5-17

17 MAY 1952

.... CITIZEN, DO YOU KNOW WHY A HOLDUP MAN CAN SO EASILY STOP YOU ON A DARK STREET, SLUG YOU IN THE HEAD AND TAKE YOUR MONEY?

IT'S BECAUSE HE HAS HAD THE DIRTY DEAL ALL PLANNED AND SET UP WHILE YOU HAVE BEEN GOING ABOUT YOUR BUSINESS, OBEYING THE RULES; TRYING TO JUSTIFY YOUR EXISTENCE WITHOUT PUSHING ANYBODY AROUND... SO HE HAS YOU OFF YOUR BALANCE — AND A SETUP...

IT'S LIKE THAT WITH NATIONS! RIGHT NOW WE'RE BEING FORCED TO KEEP OUR GUARD UP SO WE WON'T BE SAPPED AS WE WERE AT PEARL HARBOR.

PROTECTION MEANS PEOPLE...NOT A GANG OF PROFESSIONAL TOUGH GUYS, BUT YOUR NEIGHBORS AND FRIENDS WHO GOT THE NOD TO GO OUT AND STAND A TOUR OF GUARD DUTY WHILE YOU MIND THE STORE AND GET YOUR STRAIGHT EIGHT AT NIGHT...

THIS IS ARMED FORCES DAY, CITIZEN... EXAMINE YOUR SOUL AND GIVE THANKS TO THE GOOD JOES WHO GUARANTEE THAT IT STAYS YOUR OWN!

5-16

Copyright 1953, Field Enterprises, Inc.
Registered U.S. Patent Office.

CITIZEN, DID YOU EVER SEE WORKMEN JUST RETURNED FROM HELPING STRENGTHEN A LEVEE AGAINST A RISING RIVER?.. THE CREST HAS PASSED AND THEY HAVE WON, BUT THERE IS NO SONG AND LAUGHTER... THEY KNOW THE TIDE WAS STOPPED BY INCHES FROM FLOODING THE LAND — AND IT MAY RETURN TO NIBBLE AT THE DIKE WITH ITS PATIENT CUNNING...

MEN WHO HAVE COMPLETED TOURS OF DUTY IN KOREA COME HOME WITH SOMETHING OF THE LOOK OF THE FLOOD EMERGENCY TOILER... THEY ARE TOO TIRED TO SHOUT, AND EACH KNOWS THE DARK WATERS MAY RISE AGAIN AT ANY

TIME TO TEST THEM, BODY AND SOUL...

THE PEOPLE IN THE VALLEYS ARE ALWAYS GRATEFUL TO THE STRONG HANDS THAT SAVED THEM, BUT WHEN THE RIVER IS LOW THEY SOMETIMES FORGET THOSE WHO FOUGHT OFF DISASTER...

CITIZEN, DON'T _YOU_ LOSE SIGHT OF THE MEN WHO BOUGHT WITH THEIR BLOOD WHATEVER PEACE OF MIND YOU HAVE... TODAY IS —

ARMED FORCES DAY • 1953

5/15

Copyright 1954, Field Enterprises, Inc.
Registered U.S. Patent Office.

CITIZEN, DID YOU EVER STOP TO THINK THAT NEARLY EVERY MAN OVER 18 YOU KNOW HAS WORN (OR SOON WILL) THE UNIFORM OF HIS COUNTRY'S ARMED FORCES?...

WE'VE HAD TO TAKE THE RIFLE DOWN FROM ABOVE THE FIREPLACE MANY TIMES IN RECENT YEARS, BUT WE ARE STILL A NATION OF FOLKS WHO BELIEVE IN GOING BACK, AFTER DEFENDING OURSELVES, TO SOME USEFUL JOB MAKING OR GROWING THINGS FOR PEOPLE TO USE....

...IN THE PAST WE WERE INCLINED TO FORGET THE REGULARS IN ALL BRANCHES WHO KEEP THE GUNS WARM IN PEACETIME .....TODAY THERE IS NO REAL PEACE IN THE WORLD, SO WE ARE EVER AWARE OF THIS RAMPART OF PROFESSIONALS WHO ARE THE MUSCLES BENEATH THE KID GLOVES OF THE DIPLOMATS WHO REPRESENT US IN DEALINGS WITH OTHER COUNTRIES. THIS IS THE OFFICIAL ARMED FORCES DAY 1954, BUT IT IS JUST ANOTHER 24-HOUR ALERT FOR THE UNIFORMED TEAM THAT HOLDS YOUR DESTINY AT THE TIP OF A TRIGGER FINGER..

MILTON CANIFF

1957

5/18

CITIZEN, THERE HAS BEEN SOME MEAN TALK GOING ON AROUND THE WORLD, BUT AS LONG AS THERE IS TALKING AND NOT SHOOTING WE'RE STILL AHEAD OF THE GAME... ONE REASON THE BULLY BOYS HAVEN'T THROWN THEIR WEIGHT AROUND IS BECAUSE OUR MAN IN THE STRIPED PANTS CASTS FIVE LONG, TALL SHADOWS...

A LOT OF GOOD PEOPLE STAY IN UNIFORM TO GIVE US FIRE AND COLLISION INSURANCE — AND WE SALUTE THEM ON THIS

ARMED FORCES DAY

MILTON CANIFF

1958

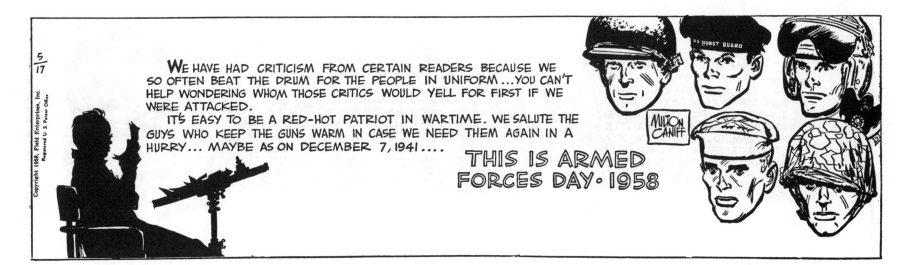

5/17

WE HAVE HAD CRITICISM FROM CERTAIN READERS BECAUSE WE SO OFTEN BEAT THE DRUM FOR THE PEOPLE IN UNIFORM... YOU CAN'T HELP WONDERING WHOM THOSE CRITICS WOULD YELL FOR FIRST IF WE WERE ATTACKED.

IT'S EASY TO BE A RED-HOT PATRIOT IN WARTIME. WE SALUTE THE GUYS WHO KEEP THE GUNS WARM IN CASE WE NEED THEM AGAIN IN A HURRY... MAYBE AS ON DECEMBER 7, 1941....

MILTON CANIFF

THIS IS ARMED FORCES DAY • 1958

LOOK, CITIZEN... YOU KNOW GENERALLY WHAT THE ARMED SERVICES ARE DOING ON YOUR BEHALF, BUT THE AIR FORCE IS UP TO SOMETHING THAT MAY NEED SOME CONVERSATION...

THE BIG JET CREWS CAN'T PRACTICE THEIR TRICKS OVER FOREIGN TARGETS, SO THEY SOMETIMES PICK OUT AN AMERICAN CITY AND PRETEND TO BOMB IT AS IF IT WERE A PLACE IN A COUNTRY WHICH HAS PULLED AN ACT OF AGGRESSION ON US...

WHEN THEY COME OUT OF THEIR 'BOMBING' RUNS THESE JETS CAUSE A SONIC BOOM (LIKE LOUD THUNDER) TO HIT THE GROUND BELOW... IT WON'T HURT YOU, BUT IT MIGHT SCARE YOU— ESPECIALLY WHEN IT HAPPENS AT NIGHT...

THINK OF IT AS YOU DO WHEN YOU HEAR POLICE OR FIRE SIRENS... THEN YOU'RE GLAD SOMEONE IS ON THE JOB WHILE YOU REST.

THE AIRMEN ARE UP THERE LEARNING HOW TO GET TOUGH ENOUGH THAT YOU WILL HAVE A <u>PLACE</u> TO SLEEP!

DON'T CUSS 'EM — PRAY FOR THEM! 40,000 FEET IS A LONG WAY TO COME DOWN (WITH NO ELEVATOR) IF SOMETHING GOES WRONG!

THIS IS ARMED FORCES DAY 1959

WHAT WAS IT YOU TOLD THEM AT THAT PARTY THE OTHER NIGHT? YOU SAID ONE AMERICAN COULD LICK ANY FIVE DIRTY REDS ANY TIME...AND THAT TIME AT THE BAR WHEN YOU DESCRIBED KHRUSHCHEV AS A FUNNY LITTLE MAN WHO REMINDED YOU OF THE SCARED STOREKEEPER IN A TV WESTERN...

AND, OF COURSE, YOUR OPINION OF CASTRO AND HIS HILLBILLY-BEARD BOYS IS STILL BEING QUOTED AT THE BARBERSHOP...

......AND WHY <u>NOT</u>? AREN'T YOU A CITIZEN OF A FREE COUNTRY? HAVEN'T YOU THE RIGHT TO SAY THOSE THINGS?

YOU BET YOU HAVE.... BUT <u>YOU</u> WON'T BE THE ONE AMERICAN AGAINST FIVE REDS— <u>YOU'LL</u> NEVER TELL CASTRO OR KHRUSHCHEV OFF FROM BEHIND THE SIGHTS OF A LETHAL WEAPON .....THERE WON'T BE TIME TO EVEN TAKE THE FAT OFF <u>YOU</u> —— IF THERE IS A SHOWDOWN <u>YOUR</u> BATTLE WILL BE WAGED BY THE MEN WHO ARE KEEPING THE GUNS HOT AND THE MISSILES READY <u>RIGHT</u> <u>NOW</u>....

THIS IS ARMED FORCES DAY 1960

.. AS SO OFTEN IN THE PAST, A LOT OF GOOD GUYS WILL BE RISKING THEIR OWN NECKS TO KEEP YOU SAFE AND FREE ON

ARMED FORCES DAY ..1962

MODERN WARFARE..?

EXCEPT FOR AIR POWER, THE MEANS OF KEEPING BULLY BOYS OFF OUR NATIONAL BACKS HASN'T CHANGED SINCE CONCORD AND LEXINGTON! WHATEVER THE WEAPONS, WARS ARE WON BY THE SIDE WHICH HAS THE BEST INDIVIDUALS —WITH THEIR FINGERS ON TRIGGERS —OR PUSH-BUTTONS...

JUST AS ON THAT APRIL DAY IN 1775, THE IMMEDIATE FATE OF THIS COUNTRY IS IN THE HANDS OF REGULARS WHO CAN KEEP THE FIGHT EVEN UNTIL THE GREAT CIVILIAN MOB MAY BE CRANKED-UP INTO A FULL-SCALE DEFENSE FORCE ...

IVAN AGREED TO PULL HIS ROAMIN' CANDLES OUT OF CUBA BECAUSE SOME VERY HUMAN S.A.C. BOMBARDIERS WERE AT THAT MOMENT AIRBORNE AND LOOKING DOWN THEIR SIGHTS—ONLY A FEW JET MINUTES FROM MOSCOW...

THIS IS ARMED FORCES DAY 1963

WHO'S STOPPING YOU, CITIZEN?

THE ANSWER IS THAT <u>NO</u> <u>ONE</u> TRIES TO BOTTLE YOU UP INSIDE OUR BORDERS!

YOU'LL ONLY BE EXCLUDED WHERE THE PEOPLE ARE AFRAID OF WHAT YOU'LL SEE; LIKE A WOMAN WHO DOESN'T WANT CALLERS BECAUSE THE BEDS AREN'T MADE AND THE SINK IS FULL OF DIRTY DISHES AT FOUR IN THE AFTERNOON.

WE FORGET PAIN... AND MOST KIDS TODAY THINK OF PEARL HARBOR AS REMOTELY AS BUNKER HILL OR THE SINKING OF THE MAINE

...BUT THE GRAB BOYS OF THE WORLD ARE AS LEAN RATS ON A DOCK—THEY WAIT UNTIL A SHIP TIES UP, ALL HANDS HAPPY AND FLUSH...THEN THE RODENTS CRAWL ABOARD AND START EATING AWAY AT THE CARGO!

THAT IS, THEY DO UNLESS AN ALERT WATCH IS KEPT, DAY AND NIGHT!

SO—NO ONE IS STOPPING YOU BECAUSE WE HAVE SOME BRIGHT PEOPLE IN UNIFORM STANDING VIGIL WHILE YOU WORK AND PLAY! SURE, YOU'RE GRATEFUL, BUT IT IS ESPECIALLY FITTING TO SPEAK UP ABOUT IT... ON—

ARMED FORCES DAY—1964

MILTON CANIFF

5/16

CHEETAH REALLY MOVES INTO PERDITA RUNE'S LIFE! —IN NO TIME AT ALL SHE HAS TAKEN OVER AS HAIRDRESSER...

...STRAIGHTENED OUT HER EMPLOYER'S WARDROBE...

... BROUGHT BACK A REFUND FROM THE MERCHANT PERDITA THOUGHT SHE HAD OUT-BARGAINED...

...ARRANGED FOR AN AIR-CONDITIONER IN MISS RUNE'S BEDROOM...

NOW EES TIME TO LET HER HAVE EET!

MEANWHILE=THIS YEAR WE SCARCELY NEED TO BE REMINDED OF **ARMED FORCES DAY** IN THE USUAL FASHION...

MANY GOOD JOES ARE KEEPING THE FAITH IN THE FAR AND BITTER PLACES, WITH THE LONG-HAUL PURPOSE OF MAINTAINING THE GOOD LIFE BACK HOME FOR THOSE THEY CHERISH.

YOU'RE JUST AS DEAD IN AN UNMARKED RICE PADDY IN VIET NAM AS IN A HEROIC CHARGE AT GETTYSBURG, SO THE GREEN SUIT CASUALTIES WOULD PROBABLY REST MORE PEACEFULLY IF THEY COULD KNOW THAT YOU HAD SILENTLY SALUTED THEM TODAY...

IT WON'T BRING THEM BACK TO LIFE, BUT IT WILL HELP YOU LIVE WITH YOURSELF!

MILTON CANIFF

5/15

Index

Office of the Mayor

Proclamation

MILTON CANIFF DAY

Whereas: Milton Arthur Caniff, a nationally renowned cartoonist, was born in Hillsboro, Ohio on February 28, 1907, to John W. and Elizabeth Burton Caniff in their home located at 149 East North Street and;

WHEREAS: This native son of Hillsboro, whose creative editorials and cartoons brilliantly espouse the precepts of human freedom, has received the highest honors bestowed by the National Cartoonist Society, the United States Air Force, the Freedom Foundation of America, the State of Ohio, and his alma mater, The Ohio State University and;

WHEREAS: Hillsboro honored Milton Caniff as a favorite son in 1953 and was privileged to have him as the featured speaker and Grand Marshal for the 175th anniversary celebration and;

WHEREAS: Milton Caniff will celebrate his 80th birthday with his wife, Esther, and friends at his home, in New York City;

NOW THEREFORE, I, BETTY BISHOP, MAYOR OF THE CITY OF HILLSBORO, OHIO, extend the highest commendation and heartfelt congratulations to a native son, Milton Caniff, and also, do proclaim the 28th day of February, 1987, as:

MILTON CANIFF DAY.

IN WITNESS WHEREOF, I have hereunto subscribed my name and caused the Great Seal of the City of Hillsboro to be affixed this 19th. day of February in the Year of Our Lord, Nineteen Hundred and Eighty-Seven.

Betty Bishop, Mayor
City of Hillsboro

Acknowledgements

Many thanks to Wilhelmina Tuck (Caniff studio manager), the Milton Caniff Collection at the Ohio State University Library for Communication and Graphic Arts (Lucy Caswell, curator), Chris Jenson, The Aviation Hall of Fame – Dayton, Ohio, James Dunn, Richard W. Rockwell, George Cahill, Cat Yronwode, Dean Mullaney, Toni Mendez, and Jimmy Stewart. The typesetting for this book was done by JAQUI'S TYPESETTING SERVICE, Ocean Beach, California.

The Lady

One of the unsung heroines in the Caniff saga is the High School sweetheart Milt chose as his lifelong partner, young Esther Parsons from Dayton, Ohio. She has been Mrs. Milton Caniff (affectionately known as "Bunny"), for 57 years now. That business about the woman behind the man truly applies here. In her gentle, quiet way she has created an atmosphere for Milt to thrive in. She has designed a home and social life that has nurtured his talent.

—S.D.

New York, May 1987

This book is dedicated to the man himself, MILTON CANIFF!